Brownie
Points

D0869836

Brian A. Corish

CanWrite Publishing and Marketing
Welland, Ontario, Canada

This book contains relationship advice based upon years of experience and observation. It is in no way intended to take the place of professional help.

The Publisher:
CanWrite Publishing and Marketing
35 Woodcroft Crescent
Welland, Ontario, Canada L3C 2H6

National Library of Canada Cataloguing in Publication Data

Main entry under title: Brownie Points
Includes index.

ISBN 0-9730438-0-6
　　　1. Interpersonal relations I. Title.

HM1106C67 2002　　　　158.2　　　C2002-900653-8

Editor:	David E. Scott
Illustrations:	Sharon Corish
Character Development:	Spencer Corish
Printing:	Hignell Book Printing
Cover Design:	Splatworks

For:

My gorgeous Brownie Point test pilot, Sharon who will be very forthcoming with bonus Points providing enough of you purchase this guide.

Our son Spencer, who at the age of 13 has more artistic talent than I could ever hope to develop.

And last, but not least, our 22-year-old business phenom, Nigel, whose thirst for my warped sense of jocularity kept me inspired to the very end.

- BAC

Acknowledgements:

There are many people to whom I am deeply indebted. David E. Scott, my editor and Lamaze coach who was instrumental in helping me deliver this baby to market. My artistic team, Sharon and Spencer Corish, who brought life not only to the cover, but also to each and every chapter title page. Pat Dracup, whose all-night design and layout sessions were well worth the effort. The wonderful support of my immediate and extended family. Last, but not least, my loyal guinea pig readers, who over the years kept me inspired and pointed in the right direction: Nancy O'Sullivan, Kevin Kelly, Ron Drennan, Jon Chesham, Lee-Anne Nolet, Mike and Judy Streitenfeld, Norm Hearn, Kimberley Cousineau, Jane Dolinski, Sylvia Bonisteel, Debbie Ellsworth, Mark Joss, Paul Mazzari, Dan Plante, Don Kennedy, Tim O'Hara, Joseph Rosinski, Robert Slute, Daniel Rodrigue, Len Hume, Annette Marchionda, John Clark, and the M.T. Bellies gang, William Thomas who graciously accommodated a budding writer, full of p & v five long years ago. And to anyone I may have inadvertently missed, here's the best attempt I could think of to make amends. Just arrange the letters of your own name below: ABCDEFGHIJKLMNOPQRSTUVWXYZ.

Thanks again -- Brian

Table of Contents

Table of Contents

Introduction

Brownie Point (broun´i point) *n.* [Latin]
Brownus Nosium Pointimus

Unless you were an altar boy or attended some girlie-man private school, you probably haven't been exposed to an awful lot of Latin. Don't panic! I was "lucky enough" to do the hard time for you.

Simply stated, Brownie Points are awards of merit bestowed upon the male persuasion for acting upon their cunning understanding of women's needs, wants, hopes and fantasies.

More simply stated, dream up an assortment of ways to please your loved one and rack up oodles of Brownie Points redeemable at most locations.

Typically, a guy receives his first Points after stumbling upon an act that pleases his mate to the extent she grants him a favour in return. Proud as a peacock, he rushes right out exclaiming to his best buddy, "I'm up Points now baby!" Tragically, the majority of his subsequent efforts are flaccid at best.

Finally, here's a guide designed to raise batting averages exponentially. It furnishes an ever-so-tasty Brownie Point Recipe, hearty enough to satisfy the largest appetite. It's guy-friendly, has great big type, loads of contractions, and plenty of run-on sentences.

Yes this book is written with men in mind, however it definitely offers invaluable insight to women everywhere. Those who study it are certain to recognize the incredible benefits derived through awarding Brownie Points for genuinely worthy efforts. So if you were looking for a book that undermines women, or men for that matter, you've come to the wrong place. Oh sure, I poke fun from time to time, but I take real pride in the fact that I'm an equal-opportunity offender.

The guide combines generous doses of humourous anecdotes, off-the-cuff wit, and rambling analogies, all carefully crafted to provide an abundance of beneficial relationship advice. It allows you to learn while you laugh, as you wind your way through twenty-nine story-filled chapters.

Throughout our journey to Brownie Point Heaven, I'll be your coach, your mentor and even a guy with a great big shoulder to bawl your eyes out on if that's what it takes to cure what ails you. So settle back, have a few cold ones, set your brain to sponge and prepare yourself for the good life.

-- Brian A. Corish

CHAPTER 1

Apples and mangoes and "pairs" . . . oh my!

". . . being just a regular Adam, he began to feel certain urges south of the border, and we're not just talking tequila."

When two hundred and sixty-five eager assembly line workers have read newspapers, gossip rags, and other assorted publications for three straight hours, chances are something has gone badly awry. Thus, to corporations who enlist my high-tech troubleshooting service, time quite simply means money. In fact, it's not unusual for a company to lose upwards of fifty thousand dollars for each and every hour wasted during a critical breakdown.

Once the crisis is resolved I tend to unwind from the more stress-laden sessions with a beverage or three in the comfort of my digs for the evening. During the years I've camped overnight in everything from five-star to falling-star type properties. Many times the most notable amenity at Ma and Pa type motels is located inside the drawer of the watermarked night stand that sits so regally between the rock-hard double beds.

It seems some fellow by the name of Gideon travels the world in search of rooming establishments laden with empty drawers and empty souls.

I have on occasion picked up this best seller and whether it's the product of giving thanks for another job well done or the fact that

I just can't seem to make it to the land of nod, the Good Book has provided me with a loose framework for this first chapter.

You see I firmly believe we can trace the origin of the Brownie Point back through the ages all the way to Adam and Eve. Let's study the facts. As a guy Adam had it all: best-looking fellow around, no pollution, no overcrowding and what could be better than a one-on-one relationship with the Creator. So what series of events took place that led to the eventual awarding of man's very first Points?

I believe it unfolded something like this: Adam spent many months roaming the earth in search of a special woman. In fact, he searched, and he searched, and he searched. Still nothing. Now being just a regular Adam, he began to feel certain urges south of the border, and we're not just talking tequila. So he called up to the Big Guy in the Sky for a helping hand and was promptly enrolled as a charter member of the very first Dating Club.

Time was definitely of the essence, so it's not surprising that he selected the very first woman he laid his eyes on. Like most relationships, things were all wine and roses for the first several months; walks through gardens, visits to the serpentarium, and more hip-jarring action than one could comfortably handle.

As time passed, poor Adam found it increasingly difficult to arouse Eve's deepest passions. So next to helpless, Adam once again requested an audience with the Almighty One.

Now it would have gone against the Prime Directive to furnish Adam with the definitive answer, so he left him with this little ditty instead:

"Share a mango,
And learn to tango,
'Cause, when things are boring,
You won't be scoring."

Now to you and me this riddle might seem fairly easy to unravel, yet Adam was the trailblazer for all poor saps to come. It must have been downright hard for him to read clues when he didn't have the foggiest idea what one looked like.

In our generation, when guys get stumped they're able to draw from the celebrated experiences of distinguished detecting minds, such as Jim Rockford, Magnum P.I., or when really mystified, the great Inspector Clouseau.

Initially, Adam struggled horribly, and with a pretty good reason. According to my pal Gideon, Adam was the very first person on the face of the planet. He got darn right used to being the head honcho, the king of the hill, the big banana. He truly was a man's man. I'm sure in his mind giving up a rib in order that the first woman could be created was plenty enough sacrifice for one lifetime.

He was quickly realizing that Brownie Points have a very short shelf life indeed. And he must have done some serious head scratching, as it became increasingly clear, that although in many ways Eve looked like a fellow human, she sure didn't seem to act like one.

Adam really started to get those south of the border urges again so he figured it was time to make a few changes. He persevered, until conceiving the now time-tested process of trial-and-error. Adam finally stumbled upon a promising situation when he keenly noticed that for the 27th straight day, Eve spent most of her day gardening. Apparently, it was a pretty large area to manage for one person, not to mention the lack of implements on hand.

It wasn't many days later that Adam seemingly unlocked the mystery. Proud as a primped-up peacock, he picked a peck of pickled pears only to be disappointed once again. Absolutely to the brink of bursting, he foolishly ignored God's one and only commandment of the time and promptly picked the apple in which Eve had shown so much interest.

She cooed and giggled when it became apparent that her man finally started to understand what made her tick. And pleased she must have been, because like magic Adam received a pair of passes to never-been-in-quite-a-while-land. That's as far as I've read in my handy motel resource book, but I'm sure most of you know what happened to the happy couple from that point forward.

By now your heads are probably throbbing from this lengthy history lesson anyway so let's end this session with a brief summary:

- During the initial stages of a relationship, "party favours" are amazingly easy to acquire.

- After a few months it becomes apparent that you now have to work for her affection, and the spoils that accompany it.

- The longer the two of you are together the more help you'll need to stay ahead of the game.

Now before we move any further let's set the record straight. I'm not suggesting that you bite the forbidden fruit that results in you getting tossed from the Garden of Eden, but stick with me and we'll explore countless ways to earn Brownie Points and put new vigour in your relationship at the same time.

CHAPTER 2

To be, or not to be

"Before January 15th, cover the bed with every single pair of shoes she's lovingly purchased in the past, but <u>still</u> hasn't managed to wear."

Anyone who has gone through the interview process with a forward-thinking company, was undoubtedly subjected to some form of psychological testing. Many times it takes the form of the "gang" interview, where five to seven staffers do their level best to intimidate you for two straight hours. In other cases you are asked to fill in a zillion-question profile evaluation.

The administrator of the assessment smiles warmly while informing you that "It's not really a test, just tick off your answers as quickly as possible." In other words don't bother to take the time to figure out what it is they are trying to find out about you.

Most people ignore this instruction and labour over the first fifteen or twenty questions. By then it becomes clear that the same thing has already been asked ten different ways, and that you don't have a prayer-in-hell's chance of beating the system. In the end you realize the company is most likely looking for someone who is:

- Aggressive, yet not pushy

- Compassionate, yet not wimpy

- Willing to put in long hours, yet not a workaholic

- Brilliant, yet not threatening

Wait a minute! These qualities sound a lot like what today's woman is searching for. Hey, just who writes these tests, anyway?

Luckily, you don't have to be a brain surgeon to become a Brownie Point Aficionado. And while I'm not going to throw some long-winded psych teaser at you, I do need to ask a few gut-wrenching questions in order to assess your current status.

Quite simply, I need a point of reference to determine the amount of work that will be required to raise you to Aficionado status. Relax. There are no wrong answers in this test; just your typical solutions to common every day occurrences.

Question 1: Upon opening a box load of parts that once assembled is intended to function as a BBQ, Do You?

a) Ask your mate to assist you by reading the step-by-step directions?

b) Grab a beer, and look cool by using the instructions for a coaster, sneaking a peek or two in the case of a catastrophic occurrence?

c) Ask your mate to fetch you a cold one and then use the instructions to light your favourite brand of cigar? (Hey, it's a well-known fact they throw in an assortment of spare parts anyway.)

Question 2: While en route to your vacation destination, it becomes apparent that you may now be uncertain of the way. Do You?

a) Pull over and ask for directions once your mate suggests you may be lost?

b)   After a half an hour of watching the same landmarks go by, you pull into the closest gas station, spend extra time in the can, hoping she's asking for help?

c)   Routinely carry an extra can of fuel in the trunk just in case another one of these scenic diversions occurs?

Question 3: When your mate mistakenly lets a "silent but deadly" slip out. Do You?

a)   Proceed to open a window, suggesting "It seems to be getting a little stuffy in this room?"

b)   Give her the evil eye, while desperately gasping for multiple breaths of fresh air?

c)   Force out the loudest, most rancid stinker you can muster, reloading your cannon as soon as humanly possible?

Question 4: While attending a wedding reception, your mate is dying to dance. Do You?

a)   Dance up a storm with her 'til you sweat like a chicken on the way to KFC?

b)   Dance just enough to keep her in the mood for later?

c)   Suggest that she join the rest of the sheep and take up line dancing?

Question 5: When she informs you that her "spring shoe-shopping crusade" will take place in late January. Do You?

a)   Go with her because you watch Fashion Television together all the time, anyway?

b)   Wish her luck, then knock back cold ones with the boys for the five hours she'll be gone?

c)   Before January 15th, cover the bed with every single pair of shoes she's lovingly purchased in the past, but <u>still</u> hasn't managed to wear?

Question 6: When she's definitely put on a few bonus pounds and asks you if they show. Do you?

a) Reply, "No I don't think so, the scales are probably out of adjustment again?"

b) Say, "Maybe a pound or two. Let's start a program together?" (Hoping she won't)

c) Inform her that studies have proven women can lose up to 700 calories during a really active sexual workout?

Evaluating your results:

1) If you circled the letter (a) most of the time thanks for the $19.95, but it's obvious you're a "Natural Born Momma's Boy" and I'm not sure anything can help you now.

2) If the letter (b) was more to your liking, consider yourself a middle-of-the-road student. Stick around, this tutoring will do wonders for you.

3) Just couldn't leave the letter (c) alone? You're one giant heap of potential. By the end of this guide you should have Brownie Points coming out of your ying-yang.

CHAPTER 3

Imagineer, imagineer, imagineer

"If this seems a little extreme, consider 'cover shopping' at the nearest magazine rack..."

Remember when Garbage Men weren't referred to as Sanitary Engineers, and a secretary wasn't an Executive Assistant? Or a time not long ago when our wonderful mothers weren't labelled Domestic Caregivers? Well, the term Imagineer is just a fancy-pants name for a Thinking Man's Man, and anyone hoping to climb aboard The Good Ship Pointorama must place the old T-cap on top of their cranimous maximus (head in the old days) in order to succeed.

Oh sure, any guy with a pulse can figure out some way to please his lady one time or another, however it takes a special Brownie Point recipe to make this a true life-skill.

A critical component of anything we construct is the foundation, so guys strap on your tool belts and prepare to imagine what women really want. And how do we go about accomplishing this task? If you happen to be a Vulcan, you simply place your hand on your mate's face and do that mind-meld thing, but the rest of us poor chaps need to travel down another path. A path where no man has gone before . . . OK, I'm getting a wee bit silly but it's darn essential to drive home the point that guys march to a different percussionist.

To ascertain what women want, some of you may feel the need to let your feminine side come out, however if you choose this route I strongly suggest stepping in and out of the nearest closet. If this seems a little extreme, consider "cover shopping" at the nearest magazine rack. That's right, "cover shopping." No, we're not fixin' to read hordes of in-depth Cosmo type articles. Our research merely entails scanning the eye-catching headlines that adorn their covers.

Let me offer you some likely examples:

1)   Gals! Ten marvellous ways to receive flowers on a routine basis.

2)   Why men can't bring themselves to utter those three magic little words.

3)   Six sure-fire tips to get your special someone to cuddle after a great romp in the sack.

4)   Picnics: wine, food, a blanket and the two of you.

5)   What to do if your man threatens celibacy.

6)   Sinfully clever tricks to get him to do the grocery shopping.

7)   Sunday sports widow, move over!

8)   Fifteen Romantic dinners he'll beg to prepare.

BULLETIN ! ! !

Last chapter I made it pretty clear that you don't have to be a brain surgeon to become a Brownie Point Aficionado. However, just in case your parents got a divorce but still happen to be brother and sister, I'd better explain what makes it work.

By reading the aforementioned "cover" topics we can see a common thread developing: Women Want Stuff from Men! Now take a millisecond to determine what our needs are based upon. Ready? Guys Want Stuff from Women!

Most couples go through life complaining that their partners don't afford them enough attention, aren't very creative, just won't share the load, and that the relationship has lost its special spark.

What most mates have actually forgotten is something we were all taught as kids: "If you're nice to someone, they'll be nice to you." This is the main reason countless Brownie Points are up for grabs; it's so simple it hurts.

I know of only one working formula for lasting love, and here it is:

No matter how wonderfully or dreadfully your day happens to go, do something unexpectedly nice for your mate. <u>Every single day!</u>

All right! Enough of the squishy stuff. I know you're champing at the bit to get started, but you must learn the recipe first or you'll keep going off half-cocked.

Your homework assignment is to list 25 of women's musts, wants and fantasies. And, what the heck! Write down 100 or so things on which you plan to spend your hard-earned Points.

CHAPTER 4

Showtime

"If you're strapped for cash, opt for the econo package. Just select a single flower and grab several of those free little gift cards . . . "

Confession:

(I woke up this morning all bright-tailed and bushy-eyed, fully prepared to write my brains out. Shortly after booting up my laptop I performed a quick review of the last chapter. Boy did I get frightened! Parts of it were so darn serious that I thought a scholar with three consonants following his or her name had drafted it. Don't get me wrong. I've had more than my share of people refer to me as a Ph.D. (Pretty humorous Dude), but I made engineering my field of choice so that's as close as I got to being called Doc. So here's the deal. If the doctor types promise not to do humour, I'll pledge to keep the heavy stuff to a minimum. Now, back to the regularly-scheduled program.)

Welcome back, got your lists ready? A bit shy are we?

Well to help you on your way, now is as good a time as any to introduce the:

Brownie Point Recipe

✓ **Take one giant scoop of imagination**

✓ **Add several cups of understanding**

✓ **Toss in a healthy portion of spontaneity**

✓ **Mix thoroughly**

✓ **Place in a well-lubricated mind and let stew until ready**

✓ **Remove, and serve generous portions on selected occasions**

Don't get all hung up on details, we'll cover the specifics that will allow you to customize your very own recipe for success as the guide unfolds.

In this chapter, and the two that follow, I'll share several of the items from my personal list of women's musts, wants and fantasies.

Emotional (mushy stuff)

a)   *Receiving flowers.*

I know when your better half gets hold of this guide and sees flowers listed first, she will probably say, "Typical male thinking." However, consider the following: It's early afternoon, the drapes are drawn and the TV is blaring as your mate fixates on her soap opera of choice. We join the plot with Jack Smooth trying to woo the pants off of Nancy Neighbour, but his nemesis, Charlie Chubb already seems to have an "in." Jack has tried his best to win the affections of the beautiful Nancy, yet nothing to date has been successful. Millions of viewers know Charlie is a seedy low-life who'll just hurt Nancy in the end. After some serious soul-searching, Jack arrives with a gi-mungous bouquet of Tasmanian wildflowers and wins the day. A huge chorus of "That's so nice" can be heard collectively in living rooms across the nation.

The story you've just heard is a tad fictitious, highly stereotypical, and no doubt seen by some as demeaning. But my point is that every romantic movie, book and sudsy opera ever created has conditioned women to equate flowers with love. But before you empty out each and every flower shop within a ten-square-mile radius, do yourself a favour and keep right on reading.

Routinely bringing home dozens of roses week after week may have the following effect:

Week #	Pts.	Her Reaction
1	25	*Nice, but did he do something wrong?*
2	50	*Wow, looks like he's changing!*

Week #	Pts.	Her Reaction
3	15	*Does the word variety even appear in his vocabulary?*
4	0	*Hey, he's wasting potential shopping dollars!*

Now let's consider a different approach. Vary your frequency and selection. Roses are fine two or three times per year. However, you'll receive a much greater bang for your buck by presenting her with colourful bunches of fresh cut flowers. If you're strapped for cash, opt for the econo package.

Just select a single flower and grab one of those free little gift cards littering the counter. Jot down a couple of words, and enclose.

Remember, the card is infinitely more important than the flower, so think carefully before you begin to write.

Just a note of caution: Don't always think with your alternate head. If she believes you expect "favours" every time flowers arrive, there'll be no mystery as to which stem will be the first to wilt.

Emotional (mushy stuff)

b)   *Just to hear something nice.*

Roses are pricey,
Diamonds are too,
A few words of nicey,
Will do wonders for you.

Okay, so poetically challenged I am. However, the truth is that we don't have to empty our wallets to rack up Brownie Points. On the contrary, some of our most lucrative scores don't cost a single red cent.

Here are five of the things that most women just love to hear:

"You're like a fine bottle of wine."

"Did your mother ever cook this well?"

"I look forward to growing old with you."

"Have you lost weight?"

"I would have never have thought of that!"

Use of these more than a couple of times per week is likely to arouse her suspicions. Timing and delivery are the most critical components in the success of this strategy. Just like in baseball there are three main components to every pitch.

Pitch selection: Take enough time to evaluate the situation at hand: What are you trying to accomplish? When did you throw it last? Was it a strike, or did you hit the bull?

The wind-up: You've selected the pitch, now pick your spot, watch the catcher's mitt, rare back and . . .

The delivery: Whisper it in her ear, leave a note where she's sure to find it, write a message with her **old** lipstick on the bathroom mirror . . . Your turn!

CHAPTER 5

Let's get physical

"Guys on the other hand, behave like they did back in their high school science lab days. Once they lit the Bunsen burner they couldn't . . ."

The second selection from my list of women's musts, wants and fantasies deals with pure old sex. I know this proclamation just made a number of you cringe. But if I neglect this topic, I really haven't had an honest-to-goodness look at relationships. So let's just dive into the subject and see where we come out.

Physical (sexual stuff)

a)   *Sometimes I wish he'd cuddle after we make love.*

All she's asking for is to still feel wanted after sex. What she doesn't understand is that when a man's "finished," he's finished! His sexual emotions are plumb tuckered out.

Yes, it's metaphysical. Guys just can't help it. But just like our female counterparts we need to become part-time actors.

Oh, I know that your particular woman wouldn't dream of faking the big "O," but I hear that many of the opposite sex actually do.

So the next time your romp comes to its natural conclusion, stay awhile. Just think about some other pleasurable moment from your past. Oh, it can be that trophy-sized muskie that took you the better part of an hour to land, or that hole-in-one you carded while playing with your best buddies.

Regardless of which event you choose to revisit, take this opportunity to cuddle the heck out of your woman. It will be a very wise investment of your time indeed.

Physical (sexual stuff)

b)   *Sometimes I wish he'd just cuddle.*

That's right, you read it correctly. It's the "cuddle" word again. Only this time we really have to dig double-deep because there's no mention of sex at all!
This is one of those areas where men and women definitely aren't on the same page. A woman can get aroused for a short period of time, then settle right back down and go to sleep.

Guys on the other hand, behave like they did back in their high-school science lab days. Once they lit the Bunsen Burner they just couldn't shut it off until the experiment reached some kind of conclusion, or climax to be exact. Women can't seem to understand this glaring difference in our makeups. But to support our position I'd like to offer the following:

- You don't BBQ an 18-ounce porterhouse steak to perfection, then shove it right back in the fridge.

- You don't deflate a spectacular hot-air-balloon before the ride is over.

- You don't chuck out a beautiful bouquet of flowers before they wilt.

- You can't enjoy a bottle of Dom Pérignon until you pop the cork.

Sorry, I got so passionate I almost lost my head! Just because we don't understand the "cuddle only" concept doesn't mean we can't play the game.

Two Key Points to Remember:

1) Brownie Points are only awarded if you suggest it first. That's right, if she has made a "cuddle only" request within the last couple of weeks, hold off. When the timing is right, spring it on her. Not too mushy, not too wordy, just a simple "Hey, let's just cuddle to-night." Then the Points are almost as good as gold.

2) Don't leave anything to chance. Think about it! You get your timing just right, you whisper those five magic words and boin-n-g . . . up goes the old pup-tent. Face facts. You're not receiving anything but grief if she doesn't believe you're being sincere. So for the good of your Points, take the time to get a firm grip on the situation before climbing into bed.

CHAPTER 6

Material girl

S. Loust

"In my haste to get it over with I managed to forget the shopping list. My mind was so frazzled that even if I'd taken that Bruce Carnegie . . ."

Now for the final instalment from my personal list of women's musts, wants and fantasies.

As this chapter title suggests, I wasn't about to neglect the most puzzling side of women known to man.

Material (shopping stuff)

a)   *"Here's $1,000. Go out and buy yourself something special." What woman wouldn't love to hear those heavenly words?*

So how do we benefit from forking over $1,000 of our hard-earned dollars, and why not start with 50 or 100 bucks to see how many Points they're worth before blowing the wad?

The answer is fairly technical and although not 100% guaranteed, the results have been analyzed and shown to be statistically significant.

You see women can dispose of minor sums of cash standing on their heads. But there's a little known shopping disorder that has ruined some of the heartiest spenders around. Once afflicted, they don't dare mention it to their most trusted soul sisters. They believe it was simply an anomaly, a time rift, or at the very worst a hiccup in their stellar history of product procurement. But alas, it was not to be. They'd been struck with "Toxic Shop Syndrome."

It can easily be explained by studying guys who wager $10 each per hole in a friendly game of skins. Any one of them can drop an 18-inch putt for 40 bucks, but something sinister can happen when seven or eight holes have carried over. Now they're putting for close to 300 smackers and the cup appears to be getting smaller as the stakes rise.

Then it happens. The rest of the foursome has bogeyed, the remaining player lines up that routine foot-and-a-half putt for par. He can smell the cash. The back swing is started and . . . all of a sudden his hands start to shake uncontrollably.

More times than not the putt is pulled, and the worst possible scourge to befall a golfer has occurred. Yes, he's contracted the "yips," and every player knows that they can reappear at any time. By the end of the month, he's probably reduced to bets of 25 cents per hole.

I believe the same phenomenon exists in "Toxic Shop Syndrome." A woman can be overwhelmed by the task of finding "that something special" with her thousand dollars. She heads out believing it will be the best day of her illustrious shopping career. Then it happens. Unbelievably, she can't find a thing that suits her. She looks and looks but nothing seems quite right. In an attempt to regroup, the same racks are examined for the fifth time . . . then, like magic, she locates it! How did she miss it the first four times?

The item is in hand, the cash register is just steps away, she extracts her fistful of hundreds and, all of a sudden, her hands start to shake uncontrollably. She quickly puts the item back, it's not quite right; she's contracted the "yips!" Trust me, she'll never again view shopping quite the same.

So how can you top this? Chances are you'll get your $1,000 back and keep the Brownie Points you've earned. Heck, there's no way she'd believe you set this up. However, just in case your mate doesn't exactly fit within this little fairy tale, keep your money, but feel free to savour the delightful little golf story for as long as you wish.

Material (shopping stuff)

b)   *Babe, would you run to the drug store for me?*

There is no request that snaps a guy back to attention quite so quickly. Praying you're just over-reacting, you direct your eyes to her calendar, and there it is, today's date is circled. Yep, you've just been asked to shop for her "that time of month supplies." Hell, you'd rather have fielded questions on morality, religion, world politics, or even your sexual preference.

The entire relationship flashes before your suddenly watering eyes: every date, every kiss, every little quarrel. Were you naïve, head over heels in love, caught off guard

. . . what? The simple fact is there isn't a darn thing you could have done to avoid it. Sooner or later it happens in all relationships; it's her "love lie detector." Oh, you can bring home all the flowers in the world, recite poetry 'til you get hoarse, or paint her pretty little toes a rainbow of colours. But this is her final test of your unconditional love. How you respond will greatly shape the remainder of your time together.

Now I'll admit I didn't have a clue how to handle this request so here's the simple truth. I just stumbled on what I believe is the most effective way to handle this traumatic experience.

In my haste to get it over with I managed to forget the shopping list. My mind was so frazzled that even if I'd taken that Bruce Carnegie, name-remembering course, it wouldn't have helped a bit.

I figured that once I arrived at the drug store, I'd just glance at the couple of items on the rack and their names would come bounding back to me. Easy? Right?

Not. I didn't even have to ask where to find the section. It found me! Aisles and aisles of products, and more selection than the largest Beverage Super Store at which I'd ever purchased refreshments. Reading the product labels didn't help, because if there's anything I am, it's analytical, and wow, there was a whole heap more information listed there than I could possibly absorb.

My solution: leave nothing to chance. It took two buggies, but I persevered until I'd picked up one of each available item.

Boy! Was she surprised when the delivery truck showed up, but I got bonus Points for effort, and never, ever got asked to make one of those trips again.

And for those of you who haven't put the guide down yet, I'm flattered, but who's kidding who? Six chapters are enough for any guy to read in one sitting.

CHAPTER 7

Job jar junkies

"You don't actually have to place a glass container on the counter, but make sure you discuss its contents with your mate on a regular basis."

It's amazing how seemingly trivial events have such immense influence on our lives. For me it was the introduction to the daily comics, or as I still call them, The Funnies. You see, when I was four years' old I completely stopped eating. Oh I'm sure it was just another control ploy on my part, but no matter what my loving parents did, they just couldn't get me to ingest a thing.

They tried everything from scare tactics to bribery, but I firmly stood my ground. Just when my ribs were becoming suitable for use as a xylophone, my father found the cure. Partly, I'm sure, by luck, but mainly because he was the most brilliant person I've ever known who didn't go past the eighth grade.

Before my starve-a-thon, we would start each day with a soft-boiled egg and a piece of dippy bread, or the meanest porridge of all time. Next, my Dad would balance me on his knee while he read me the previous day's comics. I can still remember the breakfasts, and certainly recall beginning each day with a laugh, however the only "funny" which has stuck with me is Li'L Abner.

At the same time I was saving my parents money on their weekly grocery bill, Li'L Abner was going through a complete metamorphosis. One week he was scrawny as hell, and the next he had muscles bulging everywhere. Now, that was 42 years ago so I'm certain that some of the details are more than a bit fuzzy. But I do know that my dear, old Dad convinced me that if I started eating again, I could look just like my comic strip idol.

And boy did I make up for lost time! My mother tells me that during the following six months I didn't eat 'til I was full, I ate 'til I was tired. So there you have it, how a funny saved my life.

Not all comic strips have the same effect on us. In fact there's one which I believe has, over the years, changed many a man's attitude when it comes to household chores. It's called Hi and Lois, and is definitely a part of my daily must-reads.

You see, two of the main characters, Hi and his neighbour Mr. Thurston are as different as chalk and cheese. Hi is the quintessential husband and father, while Mr. Thurston is often pictured lying on his hammock, beverage in hand, with his lawn overgrown enough to justify baling.

Most guys actually strive to be like Hi, but Lord knows how we envy Mr. Thurston! He's the official poster boy for slack artists everywhere.

Throughout the many years Hi and Lois has been published, the job jar has been pictured numerous times. We have often seen Mr. Thurston lounging aimlessly, or standing with golf clubs in hand next to poor Hi whose hand was undoubtedly firmly planted in the dreaded jar of doom.

So, solely influenced by one comic strip, guys have come to not only dislike the job jar, but to tremble in fear of it.

Now I kid you not when I tell you that I spent last Sunday afternoon relaxing on a deck overlooking Lake Erie, pulling on a cigar and a social beverage with a couple of my buddies. One of them made the mistake of asking me how the book was progressing, so I quickly pounced on my opportunity for feedback and recited the past two chapters from memory.

Now these guys had quite the head start in the beverage department, so except for a few necessary relief trips, they were surprisingly attentive, and even went so far as to inquire about the subject of my next chapter. As soon as

I mentioned that the title was Job Jar Junkies, they puffed their chests out proudly and informed me that they would never be subjected to a job jar, and that it was crazy to mention it in a Brownie Points guide.

I said no more, but later enjoyed a chuckle after listening to how they'd spent that weekend. Each had performed at least three chores worthy of any jar; in fact one fellow still had saw dust firmly embedded in his ears.

The sad thing was that neither had parlayed his hard work into a decent Point count. You see, most guys get all macho-like and make it well known that they don't do job jars, however they seem to forget that women are infinitely clever enough to grant us this demand, then beat us to death with little subliminal suggestions.

Our mates know we'll get our backs up if we're continually told to do things around the house. So they cleverly phrase things in various ways that make us believe we came up with the ideas ourselves. Before you know it we're sweating our precious little bag-ettes off with little or no reward at all.

I say bring back the job jar, and in a big way! In fact, break those larger projects into four or five smaller ones and get credited with Points for every single job. Oh, you don't actually have to place a glass container on the counter, but make sure you discuss its contents with your mate on a regular basis, informing her in great detail just how complex and time-consuming each job will be.

And for heavens sake get her to help fill the jar, because once she becomes the general manager of Choreland your mate will be happy as a frisky peckerwood to reward her poor little skunkie for any job well done.

And why wouldn't she? Her days of pussy-footing around the delicate subject of household chores will be gone forever.

So park your fears and fill that jar to the brim, because chores become quite attractive when there are Points available at every turn. Me? I keep my jobs in an imaginary piñata, 'cause every time I give it a whack, a nice prize just happens to fall out.

CHAPTER 8

This lake's full of snags

"Brownie Points can be just as fickle. Some weeks you fill the boat, but every once in a while, you let your witty little mind off its leash . . ."

Fishing is a definite passion of mine. I thoroughly enjoy drifting along aimlessly, pole in hand, not a worry in the world. Things have been great; I even have supper on the stringer. I love this bountiful lake.

There is, however, a body of water that has been nothing but trouble for me, I call it "Old-snag-a-lot." Oh, it looks perfectly tranquil, and I've watched plenty of four-pound bass jump all around my boat.

But just when I think nothing could possibly stop me now, my guard goes down and . . . twang! I've caught the bottom again.

Brownie Points can be just as fickle. Some weeks you fill the boat, but every once in a while, you let your witty little mind off its leash and . . . twang!

Knowing where those nasty snags are lurking can be very helpful, so here's a partial map of the oh-so-troublesome lake bed:

1) *Giving her "that" look while desperately trying to convince your mate that her new "doo" looks great.*

It doesn't matter if you think her hair came out looking marvellous or hideous. You've just gotta put on your best poker face. Now don't go falling for her sneaky little ploys. That's right. At times she'll even act as if she doesn't like it herself just to get you to show your hand. Just this afternoon I discovered that even if she absolutely hates it, you can lose mega Points just for agreeing with her. Yep! When it comes to her hair, there is no safe ground.

2) *Making a big production out of her one little toot, when you go around blowing your brains out at will.*

If there's one thing that's worth repeating, it's that women are truly sensitive, and this definitely includes their bodily functions. Guys believe they have dibs on farting. That's right, it's like the sign on your old tree house read: "No girls allowed!" Oh, it's not that we're too stupid to understand that gas is a natural by-product, or that even the tightest sphincter can at times be uncooperative. No, we just take it darn personally. It seems that every time she lets out a "bowel growl," it's aimed right at us, during a crucial putt, or when we're deep in thought. Regardless of the situation we've just got to fight our natural "instinks," because if we're not careful, women will be lighting off "blue angels" in the name of equal rights, and this is one battle we just can't afford to lose.

3) *Suggesting that she'll need to look for rental space if she collects one more craft.*

A State-wide craft show is a sight to behold. If a group of recycle advocates ever attended one they'd quickly look for another battle to wage, 'cause you'll never see more trash glued together in the name of folk-art.

How many uses can there be for a simple corn broom anyway? It definitely must be a gender thing, because try as I might I just don't get it. But if you don't want to be lectured about your sports card collections, hundreds of look-a-like fishing lures, or those priceless little Dinky cars you've acquired over the years, just lay off her crafts. I'm betting it's only a fifty-year fad anyway.

4) *Using her favourite make-up brushes during your Super-bowl Rib-fest.*

Some events truly are traditions, and the last Sunday in January ranks amongst the best. Others have hosted this celebration in the past, but now it's your chance to shine. The snacks have been purchased, the kegs are on ice, the big screen TVs are all tuned. It's almost show time -- 8 a.m. that is -- 'cause by 9 you and your pals start the pre-game show. As the morning wears on someone shouts, "Let the games begin!" Poker tables break out, the music is set to stun, and sooner or later someone will even be stupid enough to bet on the AFC. You fire up the one-million-BTU grill and . . . did I mention, the girls are invited too? Hey, they like a good party as well, but by the time they start getting their faces on, we're heading for stupid.

Smell those ribs! I can almost taste them now, just brush on a little more BBQ sauce and . . . Brian!!! That's right, you might own everything else 50-50, but just try being a little creative with one of her "tools of the trade," and the party is as good as over!

5) *Including any of her relatives or close friends in your sexual fantasies.*

Bedroom talk is a very personal part of any relationship. It takes many couples a substantial amount of time to talk romantically during their love-making sessions, and it can take even longer to become comfortable enough to trade sexual fantasies. Oh, most guys share the same major ones:

a) Watching two beautiful women in bed together.

b) Being invited to join in with the two aforementioned beauties.

c) Being voted #1 in a nation-wide "pole" conducted by sensual housewives . . .

Just don't let your sexual fantasies stray into "familiar" waters, 'cause if you do, all the electric blankets in the world won't be enough to take the chill off that night's, suddenly frigid conditions.

6) *Making any disparaging remarks about Martha Stewart.*

Never in my life have I seen so much reverence paid to one woman. Oh, there's the Virgin Mary, but not all religions hold the same beliefs. Oprah Winfrey, now she's one of woman's most cherished favourites, but I view her as more of a critical conduit for the passage of knowledge, rather than the purveyor of said information.

No, Martha is the queen. Women cling to her every word, and I believe its their insatiable appetite for her TV programming, which has single-handedly eradicated blinking VCRs everywhere.

Now I have to admit I've sneaked a peek or two at her show, and if that's what it takes to get a dream kitchen like that, find me a "Good thing" apron. However, I've found I could only watch her via video tape.

You see, in our house we're lucky enough to have one of those new-fangled VCRs with an editing feature that allows me to proportionally increase tape speed, 'cause she speaks *s o s l o w* that even Forrest Gump appears to be talking like Mr. Ed on "bennies."

Now I've been allowed to take some literary licence to poke good-natured fun at the revered one, but you'll find no excuse is acceptable for attempting to tarnish her ever-so-shiny coat of armour.

I know it's a big lake, and undoubtedly some Points are damn well worth sacrificing for that special dig, but be careful not to slide back to the days of one handed pe-knuckle.

CHAPTER 9

Shopping for Points at a Dollar store

"Some of the best rewards come via simple thoughtfulness, because any plug can look like Joe Romance at the beginning of a relationship."

That's right, a Dollar Store. There are no hidden psychological meanings, brain-splitting concepts to digest, or high-powered formulae to write on the cuff of your sleeve. We're just going shopping.

But a Dollar Store? Yeah, I know it's filled with junk nobody else could sell, but hidden amongst the unwanted are some unique little treasures. It's like you've discovered the whereabouts for hundreds of prototypes left over from a Poor-Man's Invention Convention. Women call them gadgets, and if you browse through their kitchen drawers you'll see that they just can't seem to get enough of them.

Of course there are plenty of other stand-by items available that I place in the category: Wasn't that thoughtful. Here are some examples for your viewing pleasure:

- Candles: scented and floating, in many various shapes and sizes.

- Toiletries: massage mitts, bubble baths, and aromatic oils.

- Unique glassware: cute jewelery-boxes, candle holders and flower vases.

- Picture frames: brass, glass, ceramic, and magnetic.

- Gardening: gloves, pots, seeds, tools, and knee pads.

- Stationery: trendy note paper, greeting cards and appointment books.

- Christmas: ornaments, Santa salt-and-pepper shakers, and festive glassware.

That's right, some of the best rewards come via simple thoughtfulness, because any plug can look like Joe Romance at the beginning of a relationship simply by wining, dining, and signing (his credit card, that is), but collecting Brownie Points on a budget takes some real creativity.

Now don't rush right out, plop down $25 and expect to win the Point lottery in one fell swoop. Dollar Store gifts or "prizes" as I routinely refer to them, work best with a short, hand-written note, and above all else, appropriate timing. As a quick for instance, gardening gloves make a much more effective prize in summer than do Christmas ornaments. So use these Dollar store delights as appetizers or aperitifs, and be realistic because you just can't buy an entrée for a buck these days, but at just a dollar apiece, plus applicable taxes, you've just gotta keep several of these little beauties on hand at all times.

Beware!

There are plenty of businesses around masquerading as true Dollar Stores, yet once you get through the doors you'll find many items priced much higher than the name suggests. Rule of thumb # 1: If you have to ask a clerk how much something costs, you are in the wrong place.

CHAPTER 10

Time, gentlemen, please

"Before you know it you're in the car, relentlessly gunning the living snot out of the engine in a futile attempt to hurry her along."

There are 86,400 seconds per day. Yep, no matter what we do this stays constant. Studies suggest that during an average day we perform 128 checks of various time-pieces.

We work so diligently to get our names on the "Hubby Wall of Fame," but certain situations just kill us. Leaving the toilet seat up is a sure way to flush Points. And forgetting to take the garbage out two weeks in a row won't earn you a tray of Brownies.

But our mega-fixation with time may be the biggest slayer of all. Face facts: we look forward to our evenings out, and whether it's dinner and a show, a sporting event, or a night with friends, it doesn't seem to matter to guys 'cause we believe that if we play our cards right the last song of the night will be the "horizontal mamba."

We stack the cards in our favour by bringing home flowers, saying niceties, and on occasion placing a fine piece of lingerie on her pillow. She's happy, you're happy, then she announces, "Hon, I'm going to get ready, won't be long," and your blood pressure starts to climb 'cause when it comes to punctuality there's only three kinds of women:

1)   Fashionably late

2)   Traffic jam late

3)   Better late than never late

And when it comes to having patience, there are only three kinds of guys:

1)   Doctors

2)   Dentists

3)   Veterinarians

(Yeah, I know the spelling's different, but they're the only men I know with any patients at all.)

Every time an evening out approaches, you tell yourself "Tonight will be different, there's no way I'm going to flip out this time!"
You grab a magazine, sit back, and practice every stress management trick you've learned. Everything's fine until the first time you

glance at your watch and then it happens. The analytical side of your brain begins to take over.

You start calculating ETAs based on potential departure times, and at first you don't even realize you've lost control. Little questions like "How's it going up there?" and "What time do you have?" start slipping out, and before you know it you're in the car, relentlessly gunning the living snot out of the engine in a totally futile attempt to hurry her along.

By the time she's ready, you're pissed off, she's pissed off and the "horizontal mamba" definitely won't be played on the all-request line tonight.

Me, I was the world's worst. In fact, I was so bad that I used to buy Slick 50 by the case.

Yeah, that's right. Yours truly didn't always have the answers. In fact, I spent many a year attending "The School of Hard Browns."

For an education in this most trying subject I travelled to Britain. I'd heard the people were very laid back, letting virtually nothing worry them at all.

This proved to be right as rain. In fact, once while I was endeavouring to locate a small country pub, I asked an elderly gentleman farmer if I was on the right track.

He smiled and said, "Right you are mate, it'd be just over the hill." Well, 45 minutes later I finally rolled into the parking lot of The Old Sheep 'n Wellies. It was a great place to mull over my notes, and except for the fact that British beer is exactly the same temperature going in as it is coming out, I had a marvellous evening.

But it wasn't until the barkeep hollered, "Time, gentlemen, please!" that I found the answer to my dilemma. You see, no matter how laid back the British are, they're pretty darn serious about their boozing.

After chatting with several of the locals I discovered that, initially, those three little words meant "Get the hell out, now!" Several riots later they came to mean, "There's time to get one more ale down your neck before closing time, mates."

Now pub owners are a pretty stubborn crowd, so if they could learn a little patience for a cause of such monumental importance, I figured my mate deserved the same consideration for something in which she believed so strongly.

Now when Sharon informs me that she's

going to get ready, I follow a strict four-step procedure, which hasn't let me down yet:

1)   I take off my watch

2)   I put away my keys

3)   I grab a cold one from the fridge

4)   I click my heels together three times and mumble, "Time, gentlemen, please."

Because as I always say, "If you can't beat 'em, . . . drink!"

CHAPTER 11

The home run blues

"Once a guy gets rolling in the Brownie Point Derby, he doesn't feel quite satisfied until he plants one in the upper deck."

Face facts. Guys don't feel real virile unless they're fully pushing the dare envelope. Even as kids we were responsible for making Band-Aids a shopping list must. We built three-foot-high skateboard jumps out of dad's spare lumber, wore out rear bike tires weekly doing power skids -- even had blowers on our soap box derby cars. In fact, I knew kids who improved math grades just by counting their scabs.

While we were playing our moms would get together and say things like:

- Boys will be boys

- They're just like their fathers

- Would you look at that?

- They'll grow out of it

Truth is, we never grow out of anything. In fact, if anything, we've become worse. Today everything is extreme this, extreme that -- hell we even have full-blown summer and winter Loony Olympics, with middle-aged men racing down 60-degree ski slopes at 90 kph in Modified Snow Shovels.

Now I'm not saying there aren't plenty of women crazy enough to join in our reindeer games, but many still have their very own very special events, that go something like this:

Summer Games:

The Great Big Tan Company-sponsored peel-and-heal bake-off.

The Seeds of the World Company-sponsored perennial/annual plant-off.

The Hairless Club for Women-sponsored wax-'til-you-can't-relax rip-a-thon.

Winter Games:

The Master Card-sponsored Boxing Day shop-'til-you-drop blow-out.

The Miss Clairol-sponsored frost-'til-your-natural-colour's-lost extravaganza.

The Patterns-Are-Us-sponsored quilt-'til-it's-built sew-a-thon.

Where am I going with this high-quality filler? Back to the title of this chapter: The home run blues.

You see, once a guy gets rolling in the Brownie Point Derby, he doesn't feel quite satisfied until he plants one in the upper deck. He flat out gets cocky! Regardless of how successful his last score was, he sets out to stage the ultimate woman-pleaser. Hell! It'll be so good she'll *never, ever* be able to forget it!

Bingo! That's right. From that point forward, everything you do will be measured against it, and it's a long, long way back to the top of the Brownie Point Ladder.

Now I'm not suggesting you abandon the ultimate woman-pleaser. Lord knows she probably deserves it! On the contrary, pursue away, however, be astute enough to involve her in the planning stage. Once she shares ownership, you can feel content with your RBI sacrifice fly to deep centre field.

So remember. When you get that urge to hit the long ball: put up your hand, ask the umpire for time, step out of the box, give your head a great big shake and then choke up on the bat, 'cause in this game a solid double is twice as good as a 465-foot homer to deep centre field.

CHAPTER 12

There goes the neighbourhood

"At first it appeared to be just a bunch of guys sweating and swearing as they worked on various jobs, but then a smile . . . "

With eleven chapters under your belts, most of you have taken those first awkward Brownie steps, and like others, have stumbled and whacked your melon a few dozen times. But the Pot O' Points at the end of the rainbow keeps you going.

You started off the season as a group of individuals trying desperately to make the team. Some came to camp with better skills than others, but there's no doubt it will take a concentrated effort by one and all to make it to the top. Oh, sometimes I've patted you on the back, while at others commanded you to drop and give me 20, but that's my job as a leader.

Recently, I've noticed a couple of you turning into ball hogs, so today I was prepared to give you the old "There's no I in team" speech, but it occurred to me that one of you rocket scientists would jump up and down like a West Virginian pogo champion, screaming "Golly-bum, coach, there's an I in both Brownie and Point."

And you know, you'd be right to an extent, because most time the game's played one-on-one. But every once in a while it's fun to play as a team.

So instead of giving you a lecture, I'm

going to tell you a little story which will lead us down the road to "Group Points."

I grew up in a sleepy little town where everyone knew everything about everybody. Some people referred to our community as a gossip hotbed, but the townsfolk steadfastly considered themselves as nothing more than extremely concerned citizens.

Although they were nosy as aardvarks they pretty much stuck to themselves, never lending a hand to the dwellers next door. Upon finishing college I moved to a rural setting. One with farms and streams and farms and deer and farms and . . . I got my initiation to country living during my second day in town, when one of the locals took a deep breath, slapped me on the back and said "Breathe that farm-fresh air, sonny boy!"

Now, in another location I might have appreciated it more, but we were ankle-deep in pig poop and I was doing my very best to keep down last night's mutton, which incidentally had been prepared by the Mayor's wife.

For a while I was stuck in a Tom Sawyer novel, begging constantly to do chores at nearby farms; cows a milk'n, hens a lay'n and a big mother of a goat who taught me a lesson or two about teasing his barnyard pals. On weekends I got to experience what it was like to be a real neighbour as there was always some group project on tap.

No, we didn't actually raise any barns, but did manage to build a couple of two-hole crappers, and a tractor house, although if my memory serves me correct, they called it a run-in shed. Now don't get me wrong, these folks were super nice, and you couldn't find more generous people anywhere. But I'd already developed some early Brownie Pointing skills while on campus, and it just killed me to see all those potential "Handy Helper" Points going to waste.

In college I was somewhat of a math and science guru, with top marks in both fields. My girlfriend at the time used to get turned right on when I'd unselfishly tutor our fellow classmates, and not just once, she'd get like that every single time. It didn't take long for me to question whether you could earn Points through osmosis. However, in those days I didn't write down any of my theories, and until my stint in the country had pretty much forgotten about it.

It wasn't until about ten years later that I'd have the opportunity to truly test this concept. By that time my career had taken off nicely, I'd met the love of my life, and the bank was kind enough to grant us a sizeable mortgage on a spanking new home in a freshly-developing subdivision. We moved in the week before Christmas and didn't know a soul for the first four months, but then I guess everyone else was in the same boat.

Come spring, the area was a-buzz with activity, a new foundation being poured every other day. Except for mud and dust everywhere, the project was starting to fill in nicely. At first I thought the people around us were downright unfriendly, but it turned out they were just real darn busy building decks, and sheds, and other assorted projects.

One Saturday morning I stood on our porch, looking up and down the street. At first it appeared to be just a bunch of guys sweating and swearing as they worked on their various jobs, but then a smile washed across my face as I realized I might just be looking at the mother lode. I grabbed my tool belt, scampered across the street, introduced myself, and started pounding nails.

I didn't come up for air until the first ice-cold beer was jammed into my hand, a grand total of six minutes after my arrival, as I recall. A short time later my wife ventured across the road, and after being formally introduced, whispered to me "You know, I've been watching you and I think it's really kind of you to help our neighbours. While you've got your shirt off, I wonder if you could handle a little job for me in our bedroom?"

I limped home as quickly as I could, thinking along the way, "Oh boy! it's like college all over again!" Now although the "job" took a little longer than expected, I was back banging nails and building Points as soon as possible.

It didn't take long for the other guys on the block to catch on either, and before you knew it we'd formed a "Neighbourhood Point Watch Team," complete with a captain and monthly meetings. At first we thought Points were available only for good-neighborly conduct, however it turned out they were also available on "follow-up."

(There's no glossary at the back of the guide so I'll explain it to you now: our mates are extremely proud of our unselfish behaviour, and as long as jobs are also getting done at home in a skillful, timely manner, they don't mind showing their appreciation one little bit. Follow-up Points are awarded when a neighbour, who must not be a part of your project team, casually stops by and compliments your mate on how great the finished product looks, and like magic new Points are born from an old job.)

Once the last project of the season has been wrapped up we hold a killer block party. It comes complete with a pig roast, unlimited beverages, group tour of our past season's handiwork, and paper plates. You see, on that day the guys do the prep'n, the cook'n, and the clean'n. Yeah, mainly to show our love and appreciation, but also 'cause it's so much fun earning team Points, that we just can't seem to stop ourselves.

CHAPTER 13

A team of wild horses couldn't

"I rank it as the third-greatest invention of the 20th-century, and even upon my deathbed I'll have it duct-taped to my hand."

As the chapters have flown by, your understanding and knowledge have grown by leaps and bounds. You've done your best to unravel countless analogies, and after investing just a few hours you've been able to consider a better way. You've started to buy into this whole "If I'm nice to her, she'll be nice to me" concept, but by now you may be wondering, are there no bounds, will my manhood be left intact?

You bet there are limits, and I wouldn't dare leave the "boys" dangling without support. There is indeed a reserved section within all of us, whereby no lure of inordinate Point awards can make us waver. It's a safety deposit box filled with your own personal treasures. Here's a peek into mine:

Certain Gadgets:

I rank the clicker as the third-greatest invention of the 20th-century, and even upon my deathbed I'll still have it duct-taped to my hand. Selfish? I think not. You see I've watched women take control of the remote and it's a scary sight. Guys are very casual about their channel-surfing, but gals are truly

obsessed -- empowered to the nth degree. I'm sure there are studies linking female clicking to Carpal Tunnel Syndrome. If left unchecked, it could spell the ruin of an already shaky health system. No, for the good of all mankind I'll never relinquish control of my TV pal.

Certain Locations:

Around the house I'm as helpful as a worker bee, 'cause I'll do just about anything for my honey. Most times we don't even discuss duties; somehow we just know what to do next. Inside, we share the kitchen, but I'm sorry. The outdoors is reserved for me. It's my very own BBQ wonderland, complete with top-of-the-line sound system, maxi-bar, spice emporium and humidor. It doesn't seem to matter whether I'm quickly flipp'n a few 'burgs or spending hours viewing an assemblage of marinated beauties spin gracefully round and round. The adventure remains complete.

Don't get me wrong. I love to share the experience with others, and every once in a while I'll even let an apprentice stick his or her head inside my smoky workshop. But don't try touching my grilling implements or your knuckles will be as tender as the main course!

Certain Foods:

Stated somewhere in the Culinary Bill of Rights, should be the provision that "Man shall hold sacred his choice of delights." Now even if these were the only foodstuffs left on earth, I could not be forced to ingest:

1)   Tofu: This is one texture I just can't stomach. So, if this is the Vegetarian answer to meat, then thank God I'm a country boy!

2)   The dreaded mini-cabbage from Belgium: Brussels to be geographically precise. The only thing that could possibly smell worse than one cabbage boiling, is a gaggle of the afore-mentioned little devils.

3)   Anything refried: As long as I've got one tooth left in my head, I'll elect to chew my own food, thank you very much! Rule of

Thumb #2: if it looks like it's been eaten before, it doesn't get past my lips!

Certain Getaways:

Now, I throw away cash in some of the most creative ways you could imagine, however there's got to be a limit to everything. I've found the ultimate coin flush is to stay at a Bed and Breakfast establishment. You spend exorbitant amounts of cash for an incredibly romantic getaway to the Cape, only to find that instead of getting turned on, your mate is absolutely paranoid that the proprietor has had his ear surgically attached to your bedroom door.

Certain Articles of Clothing:

How many times have you had to fish your favourite jeans, team jersey or sweater from the trash bin? If you answered never, you're either: a) the luckiest man on the face of the earth, or, b) a finicky little fashion designer. In the past, my personal dilemma surrounded the fact that my workout T-shirts regularly seemed to join forces with my socks in their very own version of The Great Escape. Sure the sleeves were cut off, and there were more holes in them than a giant block of Swiss cheese, but that's when I consider them broken in. Now in our house if there isn't a D.N.R. (Do Not Resuscitate) tag clearly pinned to an article of my clothing, it's considered 100% off-limits.

So don't get overly defensive, but by all means retain some of the idiosyncrasies which keep us men in a league of our own.

CHAPTER 14

Pity the poor guy who

". . . now's the time it doesn't hurt if your old year books are littered with drama club pictures of you and your fellow 'geek-mates' . . ."

Listen up! I'm about to unleash one of the most powerful, yet under-utilized opportunities of our time. Caution: if any of you Mamma's Boys didn't heed my earlier advice, I feel compelled to inform you that this chapter starts out on the dark side. I'd really be surprised if you're not chugging liquid antacid by the midway point.

This Brownie Point opportunity is a product of how life has changed over the past 15 years. We no longer have jobs for life, work only eight hours per day, or have guaranteed pensions. True, our parents had it better than their's did, we have it better than ours, but for how many more generations will it continue? There's great concern about global warming, terrorism, and drug-resistant viral strains. You can just feel the:

*S*o the computer's crashed again?

*T*oday has been a total thrash!

*R*eally? You need that finished by when?

*E*xactly how much tax do I pay?

*S*o we have to work late again?

*S*omething's just got to give!

Horse feathers! Our parents had plenty to worry about -- everything from nuclear war to polio. My Dad held down two jobs just to make ends meet.

No, the real difference from then 'til now is attitude. In the old days if things got rough you just bent over and took it like a man. (It's apparent some sayings take on deeper meaning as time passes.) To what can we attribute this change in attitude?

I believe the most predominant factor is women. The more they've become our equals, the greater appreciation they have of just how tough the dog-eat-dog world of business can be. In fact they're feeling stresses not imaginable before.

So is this a bad thing? Heck no! For one thing it's much easier to hold off bill collectors with two pay cheques coming in, but mostly, we have a wonderful opportunity to capitalize on newly-accepted emotions.

It's a simple reality that once or twice during the course of a year you won't be feeling quite at the top of your game. My suggestion: don't fight it. Recognize the symptoms and have a pre-determined game plan on hand.

By the way, now is the time it doesn't hurt

if your old year books are littered with drama club pictures of you and your fellow "geek-mates," 'cause in order to maximize your Points on this one, you just have to be somewhat of a thespian. (No, the word's not lesbian; look it up!)

Patience is also an important component, as it will take several days to complete this multi-act theatrical production.

Start out by suggesting that you aren't feeling quite right -- no, you don't think it's the flu -- it's just difficult to explain. Mope around a bit during the course of the next few days, throwing in little comments like "Isn't it time for bed yet?" or "Watch what you like, I'm just going to lay down and think."

By now her sympathy glands are bursting at their seams and you'll be asked to express what's bothering you. Whatever it is, follow it up with "You're great! Thanks for being here for me; I just feel like I need a little break." She'll ask you what would help. You must not let your pending jubilation show; stay calm and simply reply, "You know, at this point I'm not sure if anything will."

She'll then offer you several suggestions. Reluctantly you select one, give her a great big hug and . . . see ya!!!

Now I know this may seem a little underhanded, but let's take a moment to review the situation.

The truth is:

a)   You really were feeling down.

b)   She's happy you showed your sensitive side.

c)   Acting class wasn't a total waste of time after all.

d)   Coming to your rescue was something she enjoyed immensely.

e)   You really do deserve a reward for such a brilliant piece of work.

Warning!

Do not abuse this tactic. Treat it as a once-per-year lottery windfall, because women will tell you they like seeing your soft side, but they really hate guys who turn into full-blown sucks.

P.S. Want to see what awaits the very best in your class? Then hop aboard the next chapter and join me for a tour of Las Vegas, the husband's retreat.

CHAPTER 15

Las Vegas, the husband's retreat

"I have a hoot playing nickel slots and people-watching. By the way . . . have I mentioned the booze is gratis?"

Guidelines, rules, and little words of wisdom have drilled your ears for fourteen straight chapters. By now we could have collectively mined enough material to open another one of those tacky little wax museums in Niagara Falls. But as usual, I digress. The eventual point is that you're still very impressionable at this stage of the guide, and after the last gruelling chapter, brain overload has got to be just around the next bend.

When I feel a "Brownie Aneurysm" rushing upon me, I immediately change gears. No, I don't shift my melon to neutral, I slam it into overdrive, 'cause there's no better time to dream than when the endorphins start flowing as freely as the booze in this husband's favourite retreat, Las Vegas.

So sit back, take a load off your cranium, and discover how I spend my version of the ultimate Point conversion.

Oh, I know there's more than a few annoyances in Vegas:

- More blue hair than you'll see during a Smurf re-run festival.

- So many Elvis look-alikes that after a while you answer everyone, "Thank you, thank you very much."

- Busloads of seniors viciously elbowing their way to the front of mile-long buffet lines.

- More pawn brokers than would be assembled at a chess factory bankruptcy sale.

- If smoking kills, it missed the eight million cancer hopefuls that have sat next to me.

But for my entertainment dollars, you just can't beat Vegas. Here's a snapshot of my typical daily meandering:

☺ 6:30 a.m.: Shake my head, check my pockets, perform the three Ss, and gaze out at one of the most spectacular sunrises anywhere.

☺ 7:15 a.m.: Take the long ride down to the casino floor, checking to see who's still trying to get even from last night.

☺ 7:45 a.m.: Walk, walk, walk, 'cause when

I'm walking I'm thinking: 1) How thankful I am that I'm here. 2) Just what will it will take to earn my next trip back?

9:00 a.m.: Breakfast. One of the three most important meals of the day. Grab a jumbo foot-long hot dog, and load it up with enough chili to get that crowd-pleasing, intestinal gas a-brewing.

10:00 a.m.: Pick up a complimentary pass outside the Imperial Palace and venture to the 5th floor where you'll be treated to one of the finest antique car collections in the world. Stop and look with lustful desire at the pristine '55 Mercedes Gullwing, listening intently all the while to the little voices from within urging me: "If you write it, they will buy it." I give my head its second shake of the day and move on.

11:00 a.m.: I'm feeling rather parched, so I indulge in my first cool one of the day. In fact, to save reams of paper I might as well come right out and tell you that from this point forward I'll be working on achieving the perfect buzz, never straying too far from either side of pleasantly pissed. Yes, temperature, humidity, and barometric pressure are factors to consider, but when you've been here as many times as I have, just set your "slosh meter" to cruise control.

🕑 1:00 p.m.: For the next two hours I'll pool-hop, catching some rays and soaking up the "scenery" at the best hotels on the strip.

🕑 3:00 p.m.: I grab a taxi downtown, pick up a six-pack and share a brew, and a great cigar with the Cuban rollers at one of Vegas' little treasures, Don Yeyo's.

🕑 6:00 p.m.: Time to grab "lu-upper" (I missed brunch) at one of downtown's many casino eateries, where you can always find a steak special for $3.95 and receive a complimentary package of antacids with your change.

🕑 7:00 p.m.: I have a hoot playing nickel slots and people-watching. By the way, have I mentioned the booze is gratis?

🕐 9:00 p.m.: Time to take in the sights and sounds of the Fremont Experience, a magnificent addition to the once-scary-after-dark downtown area.

🕐 10:00 p.m.: Cab it back to the strip, stopping to take delight in the spectacular sights and sounds of erupting volcanoes, pirate battles and come-to-life statues. One stop left before I hit the tables. You see, they have some of the greatest designer shops inside Caesar's and I never venture home without picking up a one-of-a-kind thank-you gift for my most generous wife.

🕐 11:30 p.m.: Craps, craps and more craps! It's my poison of choice. Good roll or bad there's always enough excitement at a $25 minimum table to satisfy the hardiest adrenaline junkie. Oh, I win some and I lose some, but they never serve anything worse than 12-year-old scotch, and regardless of whether I'm breaking the house or they're breaking me, the pit boss always springs for a "full comp." eating and drinking feast.

☺ 3:30 a.m.: Enough damage has been done for one day. 6:30 in the morning will come plenty soon enough.

Yeah, I love this town and if you roll the dice correctly, you might just see me here one day. By the way, if it's after 11:00 a.m. I'll be the one with the drink in my hand and the great big, silly grin on my face.

CHAPTER 16

Go ahead -- Back up

"It's not surprising that we were headed up north fishing, but the fact that we didn't eat partially-frozen egg salad sandwiches . . . "

Go ahead -- back up, a classic Canadian, East Coast phrase signifying that it's time for the mid-guide review.

And speaking of our friends from Newfoundland, I'd like to take a moment to share a short story with you that dates back to the very first time I ever got to eat at a restaurant. But first I need to provide you with a little background information. You may recall that in Chapter Nine I mentioned that my dear old Dad was the most brilliant person I've ever known who didn't go past the eighth grade. What I didn't tell you was that he was also an avid fisherman and "extremely careful" with his money. So its not surprising that we were headed up north fishing, but the fact that we didn't eat partially frozen egg-salad sandwiches in the car as we drove was downright mind-blowing.

We stopped instead at a little diner along the side of the highway that was guaranteed to be good. And how did my Dad know the food would be edible? Well, you see there were a dozen or so transport trucks parked in the pothole-riddled gravel driveway. That's how. Anyway, I remember my first restaurant-meal like it was yesterday. I had a Salisbury steak, smothered in gravy with a giant heap of fries on the side. One of the things that allowed me to recollect this piece of history was a conversation I overheard from a couple of semi-drivers at the next table. You see, while I studied the menu for about the two-hundredth time, the waitress asked these boys if they were ready to order.

The big guy said, "I'll have the bacon and eggs with an extra pair a toast." When asked how he wanted the eggs, he replied, "Let me have 'em side-by-each, Gertie." Well, that was just about the funniest thing I'd ever heard, and I vowed to tell the story whenever I got the chance so I'd never forget it.

And just in case you don't remember where this chapter was headed, let me refresh your memory. We're fix'n to have ourselves a good old mid-guide review.

The best way to summarize our work to date is to point out that Brownie Points are collected through a finely-balanced game of cat-and-mouse. Your job is to determine what kind of cheese to offer, how large a piece to use, and how often to leave it out.

The main point I'd like to make is that the process of pleasing your mate and earning Brownie Points is an ongoing one. In fact, it can best be explained through the following diagram:

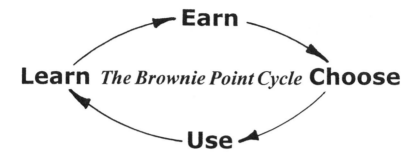

The Brownie Point Cycle

It's also clear that I couldn't write this guide without beating sports analogies into submission, however their use plays a definite role. Think back to the days when you were just a kid. The very first coach you had stressed three main points:

1)   Be a good sport.

2)   It's just a game.

3)   Go out and have fun.

If you practice all three of these, you and your mate will be well on your way to enjoying many memorable matches throughout the best of 700 series, commonly known as life. And just like in my little diner story, the best way to remember anything is to repeat it as often as possible.

CHAPTER 17

Two for the money

"Don't wear your T-shirt that says, 'I started out with nothing, and if I'm really lucky I'll still have most of it left when I retire.'"

Money + cash + moolah + dough + legal tender . . . any way you add it up, this subject spells trouble in virtually all budding relationships. In fact, there's never been a better time to look up the definition of balance than at the beginning of this chapter. Most times I start out with a twisted little story, but I'm afraid this material is so important to your future that I just had to announce the subject matter right from the very get-go.

Now for the little story: One time while I was at band camp, I met this surprisingly fun girl. I mean we really had a flute together. At first I must have done everything right, because she kept telling me that my words were like music to her ears. As the weeks flew by she started to change her tune. At first I didn't understand why, but after taking a few notes I scaled down my constant harping about the stock market club I was in. Once that was resolved we were definitely in concert together again.

OK, so maybe I didn't go to band camp, and maybe I just ran out of puns, but if you can "reed" through the lines then maybe we can orchestrate a way to beat this money problem thing. (By the way, just in case you're singing the blues by now, I never run out of puns.)

There are many ways to coach you on the finer points of tackling finances. I'm a big fan of breaking over-sized obstacles into several manageable ones. Let's save the practical applications 'til later and start by out by talking a little theory.

The first thing you need to understand is that there's solid truth in the old saying: Different strokes for different folks, 'cause what works well for one couple can be a disaster for another. Some experts suggest joint bank accounts, while others point out that it's healthy to keep some form of financial independence. The same range of options holds true when it comes to education. Yes, we're talking preparing for the real world.

You can spend six years and $125,000 to get your MBA from The Harvard School of Business like Greg did. Or choose Bluto's path and order one of those $29.95 as-seen-on-TV get-rich-quick schemes. Did you know you could buy real estate with no money down? Again, there's no right or wrong path on the road to success. (H-m-m-m, no money down, eh?) One thing for certain is that things sure have a way of changing in the early stages of cohabitation. I like to refer to this phenomenon as:

The Two Phases of Spending

● On spontaneity: Before you were sharing expenses, she just loved those spur-of-the-moment weekend getaways. Now that you're living as one, and the two of you are sharing the pot, she realizes that the word is really spelled $pontaneity. So you'd better learn how to scoop a big helping of creativity on a pint-sized budget.

● On control: Before you were sharing expenses, she just loved a man who took control. Now that you're living as one, and the two of you are sharing the pot, she realizes that your kind of power surge might cause her ATM machine to short-circuit. So before you set sparks a fly'n remember, you're her mate, not her Dad.

● On maintenance: Before you were sharing expenses, she just loved that G.Q. wardrobe you strutted around in. Now that you're living as one, and the two of you are sharing the pot, she realizes that the reason you only wore things once is that to you the laundry and garbage chute are one and the same. So you'd better save your quarters for more than playing pool, because you're about to learn a thing or two about the spin cycle.

The previous three examples deal with but a few of the early adjustments that often leave both halves of the couple wondering, "What in the hell did I just get myself into?" A little bending on both sides is generally the order of the day.

The other bit of wisdom I'd like to impart at this time is regarding the two-letter word, no. For some reason we are programmed to give this as our first response to virtually any question thrown our way. If you don't believe me, just follow a young family around the mall for an hour. Keep track of how many times the parents automatically say 'no' to their kids. Let's eavesdrop on a typical conversation:

- Little Ralphie: "Daddy can I get a drink?"

- Big Ralphie: "No!"

- Little Ralphie: "Why not Daddy?"

- Big Ralphie: "Because!"

- Little Ralphie: "Because why Daddy?"

- Big Ralphie: "Because I said no!"

- Little Ralphie: "But Dad, I'm really thirsty!"

- Big Ralphie: "You're thirsty? Why didn't you tell me? Anything for my little pal!"

- Little Ralphie: "Thanks Dad, you're the best!"

Sound familiar? Think about it, do you really think she's going to end a similar conversation over money with, "You're the best?"

Look, if you make her toil that hard for truly reasonable monetary requests, you just haven't learned a thing about amassing Brownie Points. So pay attention when she throws a requisition your way, 'cause most of the time it's a lot less work to think before you automatically answer "no" and the benefits will have you saying, "Y-y-yes!"

One time when I was at band camp I met this surprisingly fun girl . . .

No, I'm not starting that again, it's just that this is one tough subject to keep on the light side.

No matter what rules of the game you choose to adopt, several factors remain constant:

● There are Points to be had if you're the first

one to insist on making mad money a must. It doesn't much matter whether you can afford to allocate five dollars or five hundred dollars per week; there's something really important about having a stash of cash that doesn't have to be accounted for.

● When you go to meet her Dad for the first time, don't wear your T-shirt that says "I started out with nothing, and if I'm really lucky I'll still have most of it left by the time I retire."

● Don't get carried away with the whole give-and-take thing. No, I'm not talking about the two of you. I'm talking about your relationship with those overly-helpful lending institutions. If you end up using one credit card to make the minimum payment on four others, you'll have wished you read this tip twice.

I could go on for days about finances as they relate to couples, but it's something you'll need to adjust from the beginning to the very end of any relationship.

Yes, balance is the key to making monetary ebbs and flows manageable.

Besides, I really am out of band camp stories.

So I hope you learned a thing or two from my list of Pointers and if you remember the moral of the Little Ralphie-Big Ralphie anecdote, you'll be well on your way to clearing most hurdles that come your way.

CHAPTER 18

Get me to the chapel on time

"There's a magical time in every guy's life where he can do no wrong. Its like floating on a balloon. One day she sticks in a . . . "

For most couples, it's the most memorable day of their lives. Flowers, music and anticipation fill the air as family and friends come together to share in the unity of loved ones everywhere. Saturday afternoons are the primary choice for those on their maiden voyage, while Friday nights are generally reserved for second-timers.

Any old date at all seems to work for those who opt for the drive-up windows of pint-sized chapels in Vegas, where for an additional $29.95, you'll find that Elvis hasn't left the building after all.

Although the wedding day is definitely an unforgettable occasion for both bride and groom, the simple fact is that each views it in distinctly different ways. Most likely, she has dreamed of this day since the very first time she broke out her Ken and Barbie dolls.

And if you're a bride, what's not to like? It happens to be the single day of your life that is truly perfect.

That's right. It doesn't matter one bit how you fared in the beauty gene pool, or whether you are fit or flabby, 'cause on this day every single person will tell you repeatedly how radiantly beautiful you look.

For months before the engagement, she sat with her girlfriends and collectively they started the pre-planning process. Once the question was popped and two months of salary slipped onto her finger for the first time, the wedding games began in earnest.

Guys, on the other hand, spend little or no time at all thinking about marriage when they are young. They go directly from the "Girls . . . yuck!" stage to the "Look at the body on her!" stage. Some call it maturity. I call it long-acting, puberty-induced hormones.

Once a guy finally manages to get his gal to fall in love with him, life changes. In fact, there's a magical time when he can do no wrong. Its like floating on a balloon. One day she sticks in a great big pin and you come crashing back to earth. From this point forward, Brownie Points must be earned.

The winding road that lies between the time you propose, to the actual wedding day, is filled with countless land mines. Most guys tromp on so many, that by the time they hit the altar they have become totally numb. As time wears on they look to the sky every night and pray, "Please get me to the chapel . . . now!"

The reality is that until the planning stage commences, we have no clue how different men and women really are. We both utilize words from the very same dictionary, yet at times they seem to have vastly different meanings.

The first two phrases guys need to erase from their repertoires are "That's good enough for me," and "Haven't you made up your mind yet?" You see, the truth of the matter is that we really don't have much to say about the whole process, especially if her parents are footing all or most of the bill.

Our job is to be supportive, lend a few helpful suggestions and then get the hell out of the way while she and her mother get busy.

There are some universal things you need to know that will help you immensely through this particularly tense period:

- Colour is important! Coral is not the same as salmon.

- After being allowed to include a few of your friends, you have nothing further to do with the guest list.

- If her parents are Polish, learn how to polka,

'cause that's the type of band that will be pounding out the old three-step at the reception.

- When it comes to your tuxes, you won't be picking them out, you'll just be picking them up.

- Contrary to popular belief, all photographers are not created equal.

- No matter how frustrated you become, the words "who" and "cares" should never be used one right after the other.

- Don't take sides. Even when your bride-to-be and her Mom seem to be killing each other, make like you ate something bad and get the heck out of there! Remember: there are some battles you just can't win.

There are certain times when you should use the afore-mentioned defensive strategies, yet they do little more than keep your head above water. Yet this entire period of time is loaded with enough golden opportunities to mine a whole truckload of Points.

Let's look at a number of simple ideas that will improve your position in life and make the whole wedding process a lot more enjoyable. First, you have to know when and where to strike, as there are certain instances that are just ripe with possibility.

- Vows: Spend a few moments to personalize yours. You don't have to get mushy enough that your pals will hack you for the rest of your life. Just include a few words that will have special meaning to her. Of course, for optimum effect, draw the process out for several weeks, allowing your future bride to listen to your edited versions along the way.

- Send flowers: About a month after the planning starts, send her Mom flowers. Include a card thanking her for all she is doing. You will not only be awarded Points from both of them, but will be excused for a number of minor indiscretions along the way.

- Registry: Most guys dread this process, leaving all the decisions up to their mate, and then complain when all they get is towels, sheets and crystal. Get involved. Make it an outing. Flip for picks, and then tour one of those giant hardware places along the way. Nothing says you can't include a 75-cc gas weed-whacker and an 18-volt cordless drill on the list!

- Bachelor Parties: I don't understand these guys who have their parties the night before the wedding, get all pissed up and do the stripper bit. If you're about to commit yourself to her for the rest of your life, then what's that all about? No bride needs to worry about hangovers or haunting stories on her big day. Get the guys together for a round of golf and beers, or even bowling if that's the very best you can think of, but keep your zipper done up until the night of your wedding. Oh, by the way. Just telling her you think too highly of her to have a low-life/high-risk bachelor party is worth the mother lode of Brownies. Sometimes you just have to Point things out in order to get them.

- Wedding morning gift: You probably won't need a lot of Points on the day of your wedding, however a wasted opportunity is just that. Select, and have delivered, on the morning of the wedding, something that says "I'm thinking of you." and the rest will be history. Face facts. You really can't wait to see her, and it's downright hard to resist scoring on an empty net.

So go into the whole wedding planning process with your eyes wide open, and take the opportunity to make more than the best out of a very testy situation.

Allow me to leave you with one final thought: Keep a smile on your face as often as possible and the 11th and 15th letters of the alphabet on the tip of your tongue at all times. Although to be effective, I suggest you reverse the order of the letters!

CHAPTER 19

Taming of the shrewd

"They can travel back and forth all day long not carrying a piece of steel, but one flick of a switch and suddenly tonnes of unsuspecting . . ."

I used to have a dog-named Lucky. He was the cutest pouch you could imagine. Sure his legs were too long for the rest of his body, and his tail was shorter than his ears, but somehow the whole package just seemed to work.

I rescued him from the pound the week before he was scheduled to go to doggy heaven, but that's not why I named him Lucky. The fact of the matter was that he had so many different varieties in him that his family tree must have been loaded with promiscuous K-9s. Out on the prowl, night after night, searching for any old relationship at all. That kind of life can be fun in the beginning, but not very satisfying in the long run. It's a darn good thing dogs don't have any righteous standards to concern themselves with.

As time went on, I began to feel like I was the lucky one. My big ball of fur was becoming the most loyal pup on the face of the earth. And it didn't seem to matter if I was gone for the whole day, or just ran the trash to the curb, 'cause Lucky would dance up and down and lick my face like he hadn't seen me in years.

He lived to the ripe old age of 18, and as it turned out, I was sure glad I'd picked him up that Christmas Eve so many years before.

There is another kind of luck that has come my way. It gets its roots from the days when gambling was run by guys with bent noses for those with bent morals, played in smoke-filled back rooms and dimly-lit alleys.

I'm not sure when it happened, but someone in the church decided they'd like a kinder and gentler piece of the pie, and although a little fuzzy on what came first, the game or the dog, I do know that Bingo was its name.

I firmly believe that the growth in popularity of these simple, church-basement-held games of chance, is largely responsible for the cleansing of the stigma of gambling, and its move to social acceptance by millions of people across the world.

In fact it got so darn accepted that the government decided to grab a piece of the action. Luckily for guys, we now have an unending pool of Brownie Points for the investment of a measly $1 per week.

You see, nothing strains an otherwise successful relationship as quickly as a visit to your mother-in-law's place of residence. You keep your guard up constantly, 'cause you know sooner or later you'll say something which is sure to drain the old Point fund, and we all know that doesn't take much effort.

I liken mom-in-laws to those giant crane magnets you see at scrap metal yards. They can travel back and forth all day long not carrying a single piece of steel, but one flick of a switch and suddenly tonnes of unsuspecting metal are firmly secured to the bottom of the magnet.

All too often we've watched our beloved Points fly from us to her with a simple flap of our gums. I know guys who have worn aluminum foil under their clothes in an attempt to break her magnetic field, but up until now nothing has been successful.

Thanks to the Government's newest hidden tax, we now possess the means for the perfect defence, and a pretty impressive offence as well. You guessed it, the Lottery!

Now I have to admit that in the first six months of playing I won a stunning grand total of $10, which prompted me to use my math background in combinations and permutations to calculate my chances of winning.

At first I was extremely discouraged to see that single-ticket odds were greater than 13-million-to-1, but I derived so much pleasure from dreaming how we'd use the money that after a while winning didn't seem quite as important. The bigger the jackpot, the larger the dreams, and when it got really huge, boy could I get generous with my imaginary winnings.

As long as I was spending money I didn't even own, it seemed only fitting that my wife's mother should be included. Now each time we get together I quickly inform her of this week's Jackpot total and dream aloud about what I'd do for her if we got lucky enough to win. It turns out that nothing softens a mother's outer shell more effectively than seeing her daughter with a kind and generous young man.

So buy yourself a ticket this week and start tossing plenty of potential Lotto cash around, 'cause everyone will be pleased as punch and hey! You just never know.

CHAPTER 20

Lighten up Francis

"You can't even turn on the tube without having fifteen so-called experts giving advice on everything from acne to zymurgy."

It has come to my attention that some of you guys are promoting this book as a relationship self-help bible. Groups of you have started local chapters, with teams scouring neighbourhoods in search of wavering souls. Knocking at doors in your Sunday best, thumping your guides at every opportunity.

There's no point in denying it, 'cause guys named Joe have witnessed it everywhere.

Now I know this monologue is a bit of a stretch, even for me, but someone's got to take a stand against all the high-tech psycho-babble fluff that's being written these days. Oh, there are plenty of people who legitimately need help out there, but when therapists and personal trainers become the two fastest-growing professions, it's time for a reality check.

We live in an age where people over-analyze everything. You can't even turn on the tube without having fifteen so-called experts giving advice on everything from acne to zymurgy.

Well, I for one believe we take ourselves far too seriously. If every couple started out the day with a good-morning **K.I.S.S.** (Keep It Simple Sweetheart), relationships would be infinitely easier. Unfortunately, most times we forget it takes two to tango, and spend countless hours on issues that deal predominantly with only half of the couple.

Let's do a little analyzing of our own, on some of today's hot subjects:

- **You can't love someone else until you love yourself.**

  Now when hearing this, I just have to chuckle. It brings back mass memories of my Mom banging on my door screaming, "Stop doing that or you'll go blind! Just look at old bachelor Bob; he's got glasses as thick as pop bottles."
  Just when do you know you are in love with yourself anyway, and how do you get there?
  Do you buy yourself gifts, have romantic dinners for one, or stand down-wind so you can whisper sweet nothings to yourself?
  Keep it up for too long, and the only relationship you'll find yourself enjoying is with the Palm sisters.

- **I've got issues.**

  I'm the king of issues! In fact my office is stacked to the rafters with them. Will I get to all of them? Not likely. Will it make me less of a person? I think not. Although I'm definitely disappointed that I've got four Playboys staring me in the face that I haven't had a chance to study yet.
  Life is quite similar. There are always new issues coming along. Sometimes it really pays to leave some of those lesser ones planted firmly on the shelf.

- **My self-esteem is low.**

  Enough with your obsession with self-pity. As long as you continue to live in the world of a one-horse merry-go-round, you'll never build anything. Here's a clue for you. Take a walk through the wards of a geriatric hospital and look at the faces of the volunteers. Now there's self-esteem. You see, the fastest way to feel good about yourself is to do something nice for someone else.

- **I've got to find myself.**

  Again with the search party for one. What's to find? Buy a mirror, comb your hair, and have a nice day, 'cause the only thing I've ever found by turning over rocks are slugs and the world's already uncovered plenty of them.

  So remember, a good relationship really isn't that hard to foster. Keep things simple, don't over-analyze every last thing your mate says and does, and for God's sake Lighten up, Francis!

CHAPTER 21

The FOs have landed

"But ultimately it's the on-going variety of excuses they have to concoct which sucks their will to live."

No, not UFOs! FOs -- Family Obligations! Just when you've been collecting Brownie Points at every turn, your mate tosses a monkey wrench into the works by announcing the date of her Family Reunion. Drats! In the past you had nothing to lose by blowing this dreaded day off; hell you were in the big puppy house for men most of the time anyway.

This time you've got a true dilemma on your hands: should I Stay or should I Go?

On the downside, It wouldn't be so bad if her family acted like in-laws, but they're like being with a world of out-laws, where:

- The only wings on roofs you'll see come in various shapes, sizes and colours of toupées.

- There's always a group of mid-fiftyish brothers arguing who has the most money.

- You tire of hearing, "It's only fun 'til someone loses an eye."

- The buffet table is littered with more Jell-O molds than you have patience on your best day.

The black sheep of the family has even more wool this year.

Look! Sixty pounds later her French aunt still wears her high-fashion bikini.

The roast beef is so dry you need a diamond-tipped saw to cut through it.

It's been 18 years, but her bunch still take side bets on whether you'll be around for the next reunion.

On the upside:

Maybe, if I . . .

They're not so bad once . . .

Time flies when . . .

Help ! ! !

FOs are undoubtedly one of man's most troubling quandaries. The options regarding them are as follows:

1)   If you choose to Stay at home, open your safety deposit box and leave the lid off, 'cause your Points will go marching back to her like army ants heading home after a convincing victory.

2)   Choosing to Go to one FO and Stay for another has serious consequences associated with it. You'd like to assume that Brownie Points would be awarded for the Go occasions and subtracted for the Stays, however that's not how it works. When you reserve the right to pick and choose, women feel like they've died and gone to limbo. Now, they can handle purgatory, because it's just a matter of time before they'll be passing through the pearly white gates. Limbo is a whole new ball game. It's the uncertainty that kills them, never quite knowing when you'll grace them next with your presence. But ultimately, it's the on-going variety of excuses they have to concoct, which sucks their will to live:

•   He had to work OT today

- The sewer pipe backed up; what a mess!

- Our dog's about to have puppies

- He's at a Mennonite barn-raising

- It's the Big Brothers' Father-Son picnic

- He's having a vasectomy

Women hate the excuse. In fact, their whole moral make-up is different than ours. You see, if they're out shopping and the cashier mistakenly forgets to ring in a $20 item, most wouldn't dream of mentioning it. It's rationalized by considering the twenty bucks as a bonus for all their previous patronage.

But try and get them to spin a little untruth, which couldn't hurt a fly and they flip out! It's like they believe the little-white-lie police are hiding behind every bush.

So after doing the math, you'll see that a Stay definitely loses you Points, but the optional Go can also move you into the negative column.

3) The only option that insures you will receive guaranteed Points is an announcement of Unconditional Go. That's right. If you want to keep the Points

rolling, you have to change your mind set. Liken it to a NFL head coach. His team has played aggressively on both sides of the ball for 3 ½ quarters. They've managed to rack up a 14-point advantage, but something sinister happens in the remaining moments of the game. The coach knows full well what got them the lead, however he can't get the two most useless words in football out of his head: Prevent Defence, and any true fan knows that without a doubt the only thing it prevents is the win.

Unlike the coach, you have to commit to stay with what's got you here.

You might think that once a Go is a guaranteed thing, your mate won't be dishing out Points for future FOs. But it's the delivery of the Go commitment and subsequent reinforcement that pays great dividends.

Instead of fighting your mate over a Family Obligation, inform her that you've decided that from here on out you'll be attending all FOs. No, they won't be all fun and games, but you trust she'll keep the time of exposure per event in mind. It's your family, we're a couple . . . say no more.

Now she won't believe her ears, so it's critical to treat pending FOs equally as decisively, with the odd reminder of your commitment thrown in.

Trust me when I tell you that once you've made the Go Commitment, life gets substantially easier for both of you.

In the past she knew you would say no to most of her requests, so she hit you with every possible one. In future, she'll repay your actions by culling out many non-obligatory functions. The simple truth is that she's probably not jumping up and down with joy to celebrate the 10th anniversary of her uncle Sal's early release from the State Pen anyway, so you become her guilt-relief-valve for all borderline obligations.

As an added bonus, you are now eligible to collect bragging Points. It turns out that flocks of annoyed "single" women will start lining up to ask your mate how she got you to come? Each time she provides the answer . . . Ka-ching!

CHAPTER 22

Shelf life

"Did you turn and walk away thinking they can't outsmart me? Hell no! You're a guy. There was no leaving 'til you blew 50 bucks . . ."

The more astute we become at earning Brownie Points, the greater the urge to hoard; it's simply hereditary. Our parents are the perfect teachers, always putting a little something away for a rainy day.

Their problem is finding a reasonable balance. The better they become at saving, the harder they find it to spend. In the end they'll have put so much away that it will take a Noah-like rainfall to cash the stash.

For guys of this generation I'd like to suggest the following: **"Brownie Points are like Skee-Ball Tickets."** You know. That addictive amusement park bowling game that substitutes hooped holes for pins.

Yeah, think about it for a moment. The first time you scored enough points, a sign reading **"Winner"** started flashing on and off, and out popped a couple of tickets. You rushed right over to the redemption counter, with eyes as big as beer-swollen coasters, to view the spectacular array of available gifts.

Then you saw the number of tickets it took to buy anything you could find at a yard sale for a nickel. Reality set in. How much crap could they give away by charging a quarter per game anyway?

Did you turn and walk away thinking "They can't outsmart me?"

Hell no! You're a guy. There was no leaving 'til you blew 50 bucks to win your gal one of those marvellous buck-fifty prizes!

Cashing in your Brownie Points is very similar to playing Skee-Ball. Sometimes you see something you want for a lesser number of Points and trade them in on the spot; other times you stash them away in your mental shoe box waiting for more valuable booty.

However, Brownie Points should be treated as a renewable resource. In fact, they should come with a Best-Before Date. What you need to understand is that your mate doesn't begrudge doling Points out at the appropriate time, but her memory is short term at best.

So, in the case of your Brownie Points, try to resist from acting upon some of your parent's most trusted pearls of wisdom:

- A penny saved is a penny earned.

- Good things come to those who wait.

- A bird in the hand is worth two in the bush.

- You can't get back tomorrow what you've spent today.

- A fool and his money are easily parted.

On the other hand, you must resist becoming a Point-a-holic, cashing in Points at every conceivable opportunity. Oh, I know the rush you feel when you have Points in hand, but give your poor mate a break.

Recent studies have suggested that certain people may be born pre-disposed to excessive drinking, gambling, or obesity. Now I'm certainly in no position to tackle the aforementioned conditions, however I can provide you with some early warning signals of Point-a-holism:

- You purchase a little Brown book just for keeping track of Points.

- You start asking your wife, "How'd you like that?" fifty times per day.

- You begin referring to yourself as the "Brown-meister."

- You can't get to sleep without having your new Toys For Big Boys catalogue under your pillow.

- You start dreaming exclusively in Brown and white.

Yes, balance is the key. It takes time to get a handle on the shelf life of your Brownies, but don't be intimidated. Just rely on the historically-proven method of trial and error. Within no time you'll be trading Points like a full-time broker.

CHAPTER 23

In this corner

"I certainly realized that if we were ever going to put on the gloves again it wasn't going to be about something nearly as stupid."

This morning's session found me travelling a considerable distance back through time. The memory is a little personal, but I'm pretty much an open book, so you're welcome to sneak a peek.

Although she was a very social person, the first recollection I have of my mother interacting with outsiders was on a day just after my fifth birthday.

I thought there must have been a big old bug at the bottom of her guest's tea-cup, 'cause Mumsy sure was staring at it with all her might. I expected her to say "Sorry about that, Mavis," then fish out the little critter so they could get on with their gossip. Instead, my Mom started speaking to the cup, and we're not talking "Bad spider, get the heck out of there!"

No, she began telling her friend things that she saw about riches, love and even the possibility of a trip to Paris. When there was nothing left to "see," they started the whole process over again. As soon as the pouring was complete, I clearly remember my mother saying "Quick, drink the bubbles, they represent money!" I was amazed and confused all in the same breath.

As soon as the session ended I tugged on my Mother's skirt and asked her what the heck had just happened. She quickly informed me that she had "The Gift." Well, no matter how hard she tried to explain the whole tea-leaf deal, I just didn't get it, but by then my 20-minute attention span was well into overtime.

I simply stored her words of wisdom in the that's-really-weird section of my brain, and then proceeded to grab a handful of cookies.

I didn't think an awful lot about it again until I saw my first ad for something I call The Psychic Fools Nutwork. Now, I'm usually asleep by midnight, but at 1:30 in the morning I was still glued to the set. I watched dumbfounded as a woman dressed in her very best carnie side-show getup sat proudly in front of an old wooden desk. She wore beads, flowing veils and some really elaborate headgear. The only thing missing from the scene was a crystal ball, and of course the sign reminding people not to miss The Man-Eating-Chicken.

She spoke with the phoniest accent I'd ever heard, all the while dishing out sample readings to people on the other end of the phone.

Every so often the producer of the Infomercial marched out a number of "clients" who swore up and down that their psychic was amazingly accurate, and that they could hardly wait to call again. I was absolutely astounded by the predictions and guidance that was being tossed around. I mean, we're talking the makings of substantial life-changing material here.

I envisioned a whole rash of folks abandoning their double-wides, packing the ½-ton to the hilt, and hitting the road in whatever direction they'd just been pointed. I was even more astounded by the tid-bits of information that routinely scrolled across the bottom of the screen.

First was the really teensy, weensy, disclaimer announcing that the whole program was For Entertainment Purposes Only, and secondly that the price for said entertainment was $4.99 per minute, (average length of call 18 minutes.) Man, if movie theatres charged similar rates it would cost a grand just to catch a flick for two, not including the outrageous prices at the concession stand. But then I guess that's why they call it "fortune" telling!

When I need a dose of stellar advice I choose a form that comes free for the taking every day of the week via virtually any old newspaper. In fact, I wouldn't dream of starting my morning without looking to see which of life's hurdles lies lurking in the wings. I just slide my eyes down the page until I hit Pisces, then work my way back up to Sharon's sign, Virgo. Once complete, I'm good to go.

By now you may be wondering, how can he possibly tie the previous rant into anything remotely related to Points, and will he ever be able to get that tongue out of his cheek?

Well, I confidently predict that if you bear with me for a short while longer it will be well worth the wait. And even if my prophecy doesn't turn out to be bang-on, just count your lucky stars that I'm not charging you by the minute!

The fact of the matter is that this chapter deals extensively with fighting, quarrelling, quibbling, squabbling, bickering or whatever you choose to call it. Just think for a moment about the enormous time average couples waste, arguing throughout their relationship.

There's an older couple we know by the name of Harold and Maude, who routinely spend a minimum of 50% of every waking moment clawing at each other's throat. Sometimes they're relatively quiet, but mostly they do their level best to out-loud each other. To them it's purely a sport, but I consider it one of the strangest love stories of our time.

Even when they've exhausted one nit-picky little subject, they manage to start a new one within moments. And it doesn't seem to be an age thing, 'cause I've heard many a young couple following the same twisted recipe for romance. Except for the potential of a post-fight frolic, I just don't get it.

The closest my wife and I ever got to staging a real barn-burner, was eighteen years ago. I think it had something to do with a cat and the BBQ, however to the best of my recollection I don't believe one had anything to do with the other. I do remember how much energy the "discussion" took, and the rotten feeling it left in my guts.

And I certainly realized that if we were ever going to put on the gloves again it wasn't going to be about something nearly as stupid. But what does all this psychic/horoscope talk have to do with this subject?

Well I for one believe that the best way to stay out of the ring is to know what makes the two of you tick. As silly as it may sound, most people don't fall far from the star under which they were born. So I suggest you begin your research by picking up one of those 99-cent treasures that adorn the magazine racks of virtually any grocery store check-out.

Oh, you don't have to memorize every little detail about the sign of the person you are involved with. In fact, there are only three or four pertinent aspects of their personality to which you need pay attention. The key is to know your self, and which of her traits will compliment yours.

For example, if you are searching for someone with a really powerful sex drive, you may want to hook up with a Scorpio. Now I didn't actually have to research that piece of information, 'cause in another life I dated a couple or three women who were born between October 23rd and November 21st. Man, were they wild! On the other hand, now that I think about it, maybe they were just redheads. Anyway, I think you're starting to get my drift.

Still, for those of you who can't stand to give up your Friday Night Fights, I suggest you study The Brownie Point Rules of the Ring:

● Give and take doesn't mean, she gives and you take!

- Sticks and stones may break some bones but names will always hurt her.

- Sorry really isn't a four-letter word.

- No matter how well you protect yourself, low blows really do hurt.

- Once the fight is over, the no-mope rule goes into effect.

On the other hand, if you want to play on my team, all you have to do is practice the main concept I've worked relentlessly to drill into your heads: "If you're nice to someone, they'll be nice to you."

Remember, it's the main reason countless Brownie Points are up for grabs. It's so simple it hurts. So the next time the two of you are out strolling, hand-in-hand, and come across a couple that are in the midst of a heated argument, just give her fingers a gentle squeeze and the old Point fund will be treated to a great big bonus.

And guys. Any time you're fighting, you're not earning!

www.sports.calm

"How many times have you been totally absorbed watching your favourite team in action when they pull . . . "

Throughout this guide there have been a myriad of golf, baseball, and football narratives. Were these athletic references just coincidence, or was there a particular reason for their inclusion? And can a male author truly delve into the composition of relationships without dissecting the monumental effect jock behaviour has on short- and long-term Point acquisition?

The answers to these critical inquiries will undoubtedly assist borderline aficionados with the tools to vault themselves to the next level. Those pine-riding days will be over forever. Pretty intense stuff isn't it?

Sooner or later I had to come clean and admit that at one time a stint of technical writing paid the bills at the Corish household. Every once in a while I catch myself speaking like a really intense investigative reporter for those hour-long news magazines whose sole purpose seems to be to scare the b'Jesus out of the viewing public. It takes a very specific personality to feed on doom and gloom night after night without eventually moving towards total cynicism or even worse, a lifelong career in politics.

What's this got to do with sports, and why the heavy subject matter? Heck, when it comes to games, real guys don't think at all. We just enjoy, enjoy, enjoy.

My point exactly. All week long we break our necks trying to amass Brownies only to see them disappear weekend after weekend. It's kind of like your mate has her very own Ms. Pacman game, gobbling your Points at every turn, and to make things worse, she gets an additional life for every different sport you watch or play.

Oh sure, you could be a total wuss and give up sports altogether to protect your stash, but throw out your athletic supporter at the same time, 'cause it's obvious you'll have nothing left worth protecting. No, guys don't need to work harder; they need to work . . . like electricians. That's right, the power to her handy little video game of doom must be re-routed. So consider yourselves apprentices, and let's see if we can't get this wiring diagram straightened out.

Taking a hard, long, look at this chapter's title is as good a place to start as any: www.sports.calm isn't just a clever little heading and it certainly wasn't intended to upset all you Internet purists by using .calm rather than .com, 'cause dammit Jim, there's real meaning within this enterprise!

How many times have you been totally

absorbed watching your favourite team in action when they pull a bonehead move of monumental proportion? And how many times did you rant, rave, chug, curse, throw, scream, chug, curse, fart, stomp, chug and curse as your first twelve reactions? Well, if you can't count that high, join the club, but what's with our mates dropping a cow every time we display some well-founded reactions? And how many questions am I going to ask in one paragraph anyway? Well the answer may seem a bit like poetry:

Can't you tell, football's a hit,
   He missed the field goal, and I said sh't.

All was fine, all was neat,
   He dropped the ball, I stomped my feet.

Lift your glass, have a cheer,
   Another penalty, kiss my rear.

Men they drink, men they stink,
   It's nice out today, so I'll wear pink.

H-m-m-m. One of these rhymes is not like the others!

The same can definitely be said with respect to the contrasting reactions displayed by members of the opposite sex during tension-filled sporting moments.

Most guys are involved, embroiled, enmeshed and entangled . . . and that's without a substantial bet on the line.

Most Gals are unexcitable, inert, patient, stoical, quiescent, and puzzled . . . at our behaviour that is.

Try as women might, they just can't conceive how their sweet, compassionate, God-fearing husbands, can transform into full-fledged lunatics at sporting events.

We on the other hand, can't comprehend why our mates get so darn upset with some well-founded reactions to sporting ineptitude. We eke out a living for our families by working our knuckles to the bone, then dig deep into our wallets to support our favourite teams. But I swear we'll get de-nutted before giving up the right to chastise the multi-million-dollar stars whose salaries we help pay.

And there's no way I buy into the theory that suggests boys and girls are different from day one. You always hear some proud parent stating how "My little Johnny is a true boy; why he made Va-room! Va-room! noises before he ever saw a car."

Yeah, right. I guess boys must have made clippity-clop noises in the 1600s before they ever saw a horse? Of course not! How we act at sporting events is predominantly learned behaviour.

Okay, so I've milked this premise 'til it's udderly empty, but the importance of understanding our differing points of reference is nothing less than crucial to the pending solution.

Let's glance at some typically used stopgaps:

1) We plead long-term temporary insanity.

2) We constantly beg forgiveness.

3) We offer to join Anger Anonymous.

4) We promise, never again, again.

5) We hop on the El Niño bandwagon.

The five previous solutions contain varying elements of merit, however offer little in the way of short-circuiting Point loss.

No, we have to forget about conjuring up further defensive measures and commit to embarking upon a strategy based on offence. But how do we take an aggressive position without changing our behaviour?

Education is the solution, and just like in school, the basics must be mastered before tackling more advanced studies. In sports it doesn't get any more elementary than little league play. This is the very basis for guys' obsession with athletics. And despite being inundated at every turn with proclamations of "It doesn't matter if you win or lose, it's how you play the game," show me one kid who enjoys a good loss and I'll show you a future . . . accountant.

Now, it will do you no good to drag your mate out to view any old youngsters' game you come across. The key is her relationship with one of the participants. It doesn't matter if it's your kid, a nephew or a niece as long as she's emotionally involved 'cause one of the scariest spectacles in sports today is watching a woman's behaviour at a loved one's game.

No coach, referee or disagreeing parent is safe in the same vicinity. Why, I've seen husbands so embarrassed by the situation that they've had themselves paged just so they could get away from their screaming madwoman.

So don't you go changing. Get her involved instead, because once she's hooked on minor league play, the jump to the majors won't be far behind. And if you can stand listening to her rant, rave, chug, curse, throw, scream, chug, curse, fart, stomp, chug and curse all game long your Points will remain safely in their vault.

CHAPTER 25

Play that funky music, Brownie boy

"Besides, most of the places we frequented were dark as molasses and they played that funky music real darn loud."

Writing a guide that satisfies men from all walks of life can be a very tall order indeed. Furthermore, you might think chapters are written chronologically, but I use the eeny-meeny-miney-moe method when selecting which subject to tackle next.

Anyway, after sitting back and reading the previous 24, it occurred to me that I might have neglected all you dating dudes. Oh sure, I started off with Adam, and the rest of the material isn't exactly anti-single, but the fact that I'm a mid-forties married male has undoubtedly biased the material to a certain extent.

Once I recognized this oversight, it pleased me to know I still had time to rectify the situation. I was relieved one moment, horrified the next, as it quickly hit me that I hadn't dated in what seems like a zillion years; hell, I don't even hang out with any relationship wanna-bes.

Now I realize things are different when it comes to S.T.Ds and alike, but the basic premise still remains the same.

There are two distinct phases of dating:

1) Finding *someone* who'll go out with you.

2) Holding on to that *special someone.*

To address the first phase I'll share the strategy we used when I was a part of the dating scene. Back then, we hunted in packs of four or more, and wolves must have fascinated us, 'cause we had a full-blown hierarchy.

Bill was the leader. He had that G.Q. look, and definitely got first right of refusal when prey was spotted. I was awarded the first-runner up position, and if for any reason Bill couldn't fulfil his duties as . . . you get the picture.

Being second dog was a role I relished greatly. Oh, I helped spot our quest for the night, but Bill had all the pressure of marking our territory, and getting the rest of the pack invited to the table. As for Jeff, he could always get his hands on the car for the night, so he was indispensable. Poor Mike rounded out our little group. He was graciously voted most congenial. He had a nose like an eggplant and a horrible little squeaky voice, but we couldn't have functioned like a well-oiled machine without him.

You see it was common to see a couple or three good-looking women at a table, but when the brood spread to four, there was always a likely chance that there was an early candidate for the Pasta Hall of Fame along for ballast.

Now, Mike was a realist and would graciously accept a heavyweight without a fuss. Besides, most of the places we frequented were dark as molasses, and they played that funky music real darn loud.

Now before any of you members of the fairer sex start boiling over, take a good, long hard look back and I think you'll remember that you gals did things exactly the same way we did.

I could spin juicy stories all day long, but I think you've got the picture and my wife informs me that it would be Pointless for me to continue reliving my dating days.

Let's move on to Phase Two, holding on to that special someone.

I have to admit that I struggled with this part of the book more than any other. It's not that I couldn't think of anything to say to all you young bucks. It's just that I couldn't think of how to say it in a short, but effective way.

'Cause even if you were smart enough, or lucky enough to make out like a bandit during the .com I.P.O. craze of 2000, and you've got millions of dollars stashed away, there is one thing you just can't buy: P A T I E N C E.

Maybe you're thinking that I should have included love, but if you have enough money, you can rent it often enough that you just might not realize the difference.

So for those of you who haven't yet mastered the art of patience, I'm going to leave you with the best two words of advice I know: SPEED KILLS!

That's right. Trust me when I tell you that being in a hurry, or premature I should say, is not considered an endearing quality by many women.

So if you stop and mentally place those words of wisdom in front of everything you say and do, you'll be well on your way to cultivating a lasting relationship.

Mamma's got a brand new Santa

"Instead of you and your mate racking your brains out year after year in search of the perfect gift, agree instead to give only . . . "

In your rookie Brownie Point season, you've compiled some pretty impressive stats, batting .302, with 72 RBIs and 14 stolen bases. Its taken some coaching, but you've learned to lay off the long ball, spraying your hits to all parts of the park instead. Your opposing pitcher has been equally as excited with your play, and despite serving up some easy offerings she has remained solidly in the game.

It's time for the year-end finale: Christmas. How you perform will greatly determine your value heading into next year.

In the minors, you've been hot and cold at Christmas time, playing well one year, and stinking up the joint the next. You believed the only thing that would propel you to the big show was a bases-loaded, bottom-of-the-9th, grand salami.

So you'd pull out your credit card and purchase the biggest, bestest present you could think of. Oh, you were always happy with the pitch you'd selected, and your mate's eyes would remain glued to the ball as it sailed through the air . . . unfortunately, often as not, it would end up just another long foul ball.

But enough of the baseball talk. Let's deck the halls and begin to dissect your old Ho! Ho! Ho! methods, while considering some alternative suggestions.

In the past you opted for the big gift theory, however it had some very serious shortcomings.

Initially upon opening her gift, your mate would appear thrilled to death. She realized how hard you had tried, and regardless of the item, truly appreciated the effort. Her reaction made you feel proud as a peacock. Unfortunately, it's not until a few days later when she utters those dreaded words "Did you keep that receipt?" that you know it's another bust. To make things worse, the maximum Point value attainable for the single gift is relatively low.

So let's redefine the ground rules. Instead of you and your mate racking your brains year after year in search of the perfect present, agree instead to give only stocking-stuffers, and not just a few, but 25 or 30.

Think of the benefits:

● You'll have way more gifts to open.

- There's safety in numbers. Even an idiot couldn't get 30 things wrong.

- You can buy at least five things that you'll like for sure, even if she doesn't.

- The maximum Point value goes up substantially, based on added effort alone.

- You can play some really neat drinking games while wrapper-ripping, based on correct gift-guessing. Yes, shaking, sniffing, and squeezing are permitted 'til one of you yells FRAGILE!

- Stocking stuffers aren't really expensive, so throw caution to the wind and burn those receipts, 'cause in this game no exchanges are allowed.

Rule of thumb # 3: if you want something badly enough for yourself, pick it up on your own, 'cause nothing is worse than playing Christmas Russian Roulette year after year. The real benefit of this gift-giving system is that you will no longer have lofty expectations, so you can't possibly be disappointed. It's just plain fun!

The last rule is a dilly, as it does not allow for the exchanging of gift ideas. If one is suggested, even by mistake, it must be erased from the possibility pool. The aim is to be creative; what would be the point of wildly rifling through shopping bags as they came through the door if you already knew what was on the list?

Wondering where to come up with worthy stuffers? Oh, there are countless catalogues, and recalling what she bought her friends and relatives last year doesn't hurt. But if that's not quite enough, try holding a 'tis-the-season brainstorming session with some pals at your watering hole of choice. After a few glasses of Cool-aid, the ideas will undoubtedly start flowing. Hell! Some of your buddies might even have an actual gift or two worth trading for.

In summation, have some fun at Christmas, and when you finally get so proficient that you're choosing gifts she doesn't have a clue she wants yet, you've mastered The St. Nick Shuffle.

CHAPTER 27

It's not over 'til the pleasantly- plump lady sings

"Open your Romantic Dinners Made Easy cookbook and pour yourself a three-finger, single-malt scotch, 'cause it's time . . ."

Most of us have this next trait in common. We're idea guys, in fact trouble-shooter is our middle name. We take great pride in the roles we've played as explorers and inventors.

Unfortunately, we don't like to sweat the little details. Once we've developed an idea we like to move on, leaving the bits and pieces for someone else to complete. In comparison, women make great researchers, as they possess the patience to see projects through to completion. This difference in our makeup has led to thousands of close-but-no-cigar Points.

If you take an hour or so, I'm sure you can recall hundreds of times when you just about got things right. Those darn Points were so close, you could almost smell them. Then unexplainably, they disappeared and it was back to the drawing board again. Having a little trouble picturing what I'm talking about? Let me set the stage for you:

It's 3 pm. You've left work early to shop the favourite speciality markets of the world's finest chefs. Free-range capon breasts, feta cheese, porcini mushrooms, an array of fresh herbs, an olive-and-onion focaccia, a fine bottle of Merlot, the list goes on . . .

Your mate will arrive home at 6:30 p.m. expecting freshly-delivered pizza. You see, Wednesday is take-out night, so this evening is destined to be a big surprise.

You open your Romantic Dinners Made Easy cookbook and pour yourself a three-finger, single-malt scotch, 'cause it's time to prepare the award-winning Brownie Point Feast. Now by carefully following the first instructions you've read in years, the items are prepared like clockwork. The capon breasts are stuffed, wrapped with butcher's string and placed into the pre-heated oven. The flowers are arranged, the wine's uncorked, the candles are lit, the music's just right, and the place smells as good as a two-hundred-dollar-a-plate restaurant. It's perfection! You take a moment to admire your handiwork. Could it possibly get any better than this?

The door handle turns and you can't wait to see the look on her face.

To your utter amazement she seems completely oblivious to the exquisite sights, smells, and sounds you've prepared, rocketing instead towards the war zone you've left behind, once commonly known as the kitchen.

By the time she finishes her five-minute tirade, you'll have graduated from Details, Details, Details 101.

So the next time you plan to enter her world, remember Brownie Points aren't yours 'til the pleasantly-plump lady sings.

CHAPTER 28

Guinea Pigs from Heaven

"So three months ago I dreamed up the idea of sending copies to a wide cross-section of . . ."

There comes a time when every writer seeks re-assurance about the product he or she has set to paper. I'm the king of doubt, and just had to know what real guys thought. So three months ago I dreamed up the idea of sending copies to a wide cross-section of fifty men in order to see what effect the guide might have on their relationships.

Identities have been protected, but here's a sample of some uncut replies. We golfers at Brownie Point Headquarters like to refer to it as: Fore-hmmm!

Just the guy next door:

Thank you for the complimentary copy. First, I would like to say that I consider myself just a regular fellow. In the past, I have had my share of relationships, and can honestly say that I have met the perfect woman at least 6-9 times before. I am considered handsome, in a rugged sort of way, am 36 and college educated. So I struggled constantly to find the reasons why my relationships routinely failed after just 2-3 weeks. Then I read Brownie Points. Wow! Has my life changed! It turns out I had several deficiencies:

1)   There weren't enough quality selections in my play-book; after a few hot and heavy dates I would have to revert to running the same series over and over again.

2)   It turns out chicks, I mean women, are not keen on hearing about my last 137 relationships.

3)   You know, you're right. Roses only do work the first couple of times.

Eleven weeks later, I am still dating the same fabulous gal. Oh sure, I still slip up every once in a while, mentioning a past relationship or two, but it looks like we might just make it. I believe the key may just be to pay heed to your advice about not including family in our sexual fantasies, because wow! does she have one hot sister, but also a jealous streak that could blister the paint off my '63 'vette.

R.T., Delaware

Catholic Boy comes home:

Bless me father for I have sinned and it has been six long years since my last confession. I am a married, 42-year-old man from the midwest. I have to be totally honest when I tell you that you almost lost me. You see, 10 years ago next month, we tied the blessed knot. We had a good marriage for the first 3 ½ years, then we started a family. Hormones, egos and diapers replaced the decent relationship we had, and here is where you almost lost me. See, you never once mentioned kids in your guide and I was beginning to feel left out. Oh, I thoroughly enjoyed reading it, and at times laughed so hard my wife thought I was watching Women's Golf. Still, I couldn't stop feeling that this was just a club for childless couples everywhere. Then it happened. I was sitting in my private library and I had just finished your book, however nature dictated that I stay a little longer. So I read the dedication, acknowledgements, and finally, about the author. I almost fell off my favourite white appliance when I read that you have 13- and 22-year-old sons. It finally sunk into my multi-plated head; Brownie Point Heaven is not exclusively reserved for D.I.N.K.s.

Yes, our 10th anniversary was three weeks ago, and although I have not made a return visit to the confessional, I sure have made a whole lot more trips to the altar.

S. T., Kansas

Disgruntled in Dallas:

Hey man, what kind of hash are you trying to sling here? This book is for pussies! I catch you in the Red-Necked Bar and Grill and I'll kick your Lilly-white ass!

We treat our women just fine down here. Hell, they're even allowed to go to bingo once a month. And don't go ragg'n on the Palm sisters, because us good-old-boys have been raised to believe that a man's gotta do, what a man's gotta do.

B-B. G., Dallas

Only in Canada, eh?

It's June 15th and I'm just packing away my skis for the season. No, not because we live in igloos all year long! I live in beautiful Banff Alberta, where you can ski the bowl until early summer.

We get tens of thousands of tourists each year. It's a bit pricey, so some people have to save a while to get here, and then there's Laura; 31 years' old, absolutely gorgeous and loaded. She comes from a long line of Connecticut millionaires, and has dated only those within her circles. Guys with names like Biff and Blaine who received 930 Porsche Whale-tails when they turned 18, and who throughout their 20s and early 30s acquired more additional chick-magnets than I could put on a thousand bar fridges.

Now, I do all right for myself; a decent job, a one-bedroom condo at the base of the slopes and a modest, but well-balanced stock portfolio. Still, until reading your guide, I would not have dreamed of pursuing her. Upon digesting it, I gambled that after dating a steady diet of stuffy rich boys, none that had less than The 3rd following their pompous, little family names, that she would be starving for a lean, mean, dating machine. One who would capture her heart with cleverness and constant variety; putting aside the $10G tennis bracelet type gifts, for cute little stuffed toy chipmunks and the like. I can tell you that for the past six weeks we have been inseparable, and she is even starting to take a shine to getting her fingers sticky while she eats.

Her mother is flying in next weekend and I hear she will be a tough nut to crack. So, pardon me while I re-read my guide and design a method of shifting the old gal from a steady diet of premium cashews, to the occasional bowl full of fresh Canadian beer nuts.

F. G., Calgary

Mamma's boy strikes Bronze:

It is very tough going through life in the shadow of your Mom. Learning to excel at chess and becoming the ultimate yes-man are but two of the pre-requisites required for achieving full-fledged Momma's boy status.

When your guide arrived with my name clearly pasted across the front of the plain brown wrapper, I knew it would only be a matter of time before Mother finished it, and then I would get my turn. You may have guessed by now, that I have thighs like Richard Simmons, and reside in my mother's basement apartment with my wife of three years. She is an exact clone of my mother in every conceivable way: what a life!

I read the sneak preview to your guide and immediately chugged three extra-lite beers in order to summon the nerve to read the rest. It sickened me to see that men everywhere were being awarded Points for things I was compelled to do under fear of great reprisal. After reading it for the third time I gazed into my Barbie's

Playhouse mirror and saw Captain Virile. No longer would my kindnesses be taken for granted. Heck, if I want to stay out past my 8:00 p.m. curfew to play an extra couple of hands of bridge with Derf, I will! Now, sadly, I have to confess that once I came down from my beer buzz, I realized that my Captain Virile mask is now reserved only for times when my mother and wife go out, but "Damn it Jim, it's a start!"

P.R., Ma.

Want to see your letter published in "Fore-hmmm," or just read more drivel from guys just like you? Turn to page 188 for an exciting Brownie Point Newsletter offer.

CHAPTER 29

El Finito

"The guide allowed you to gather helpful hints along the meandering path to 'Brownie Point Heaven,' while learning . . ."

A couple of decades ago I was the honorary president of the Big Toys for Big Boys Club. Some of my buddies were heavily into tools, while for others fishing was their passion. But for me, if it had a motor, I just had to have one or more. My collection included bikes, boats, snowmobiles, and cars. Now just in case you think that size doesn't matter, I'm here to advise you to give your head a great big shake. Quite simply, horsepower rules!

I had some real nice rides, but without a doubt my favourite toy of the time was a '66 El Camino. She was the proud possession of Pete, a good friend of mine. And was powered by a blueprinted 396-cubic-inch power plant, sported dual 750 pumpers, tuned headers and a four-speed trannie. Her show-finish, '67 International Corvette blue paint job was just about as deep as the pockets it took to have the work done.

(Come to think about it, if I had invested half of the money I pissed away on heavy metal playthings back then I wouldn't need to be chasing a dollar now by pounding away at this keyboard. Don't get me wrong. Even if I could, I wouldn't change a thing, and besides, how would I have managed to meet all you fine folk?)

Anyway, back then Pete and I used to go on some pretty serious road trips, where we shared expenses and turns behind the wheel. One splendid day in El Paso, I got on the El Camino's gas a tad aggressively and chirped the tires for two solid blocks before a local law enforcement officer decided to put an end to my fun. And speaking of endings, or El Finito, as he called it, here comes one now.

But first, let's conduct a little review of our fascinating journey. We travelled back in time to the days of Adam and Eve, sweated through pre-test jitters, imagineered what women want, then put some of what we learned to action in a trilogy of chapters dealing with their musts, wants and fantasies.

Next we conquered our fears of the dreaded Job Jar, cruised that fickle body of water, Old snag-a-lot, found our budget-conscious selves in a Dollar Store and learned to click our heels together, beer in hand, while saying, Time, gentlemen, please! Found out why its best to lay off the long ball and went on a neighbourhood tour, where we gained insight regarding Handy Helper Points.

By the end of Chapter 12 many of you were starting to wonder, are there no bounds, will my manhood be left intact? After some reassuring words we moved on to a chapter that bordered on deception, cashing in big-time on newly-accepted emotions, toured the ultimate Point conversion, Las Vegas, the husband's retreat and came to understand that Go Ahead-Back Up had something to do with a game of cat and mouse.

Next we made some sense out of finances with the help of a clever little band camp story and followed that up with some helpful Pointers that make the whole wedding process a great deal easier to swallow.

The remaining chapters should still be relatively fresh in your mind so I'll spare you the instant replay. In summation, the guide allowed you to gather helpful hints along the meandering path to Brownie Point Heaven, while learning more about women through one man's eyes than should be allowed by law. No, most times you weren't given step-by-step instructions; the majority of you answered   c) to the BBQ assembly question in Chapter 2 anyway, so what would have been the point?

In the end you've simply learned to lower your testosterone levels by a notch or two, revisited the rules of fair play, and were encouraged to let your imaginations run as freely as they did when you were kids playing cops and robbers in the vacant lot next door.

So study your notes, develop a game plan, then rare back and fire your best pitches. Oh, the umpire may miss the odd strike, but by the end of the season you'll both be candidates for the all-star team.

And remember, in the case of all you macho types . . . *be yourself and a little bit less.*

The Amazing Brownie Point Newsletter:

"This is your way of showing your loved one that your quest to become a more attentive mate isn't close to being over."

Have you ever wanted to belong to an exclusive club? One that is sans women yet adds to your growing knowledge of what makes them tick?

Would you be keen on receiving semi-annual updates, chock-full of Fore-hmmm stories, timely Brownie Point tidbits, silly cartoons and really neat paraphernalia for you to purchase at super prices?

Look no further! Consider this your personal invitation to become a Charter Member of the Royal Order of Brownie Point Aficionados.

Not dialling the 1-800 number yet? Well consider this: order now and we'll include a spectacular Brownie Point Tee-shirt and six really neat Beer Coasters. All for the ridiculously low introductory price of $29.95 per year. (Shipping and handling add $4.95).

This is your way of showing your loved one that your quest to become a more attentive mate isn't close to being over. The Points you'll receive from informing her of this fact alone is well worth the money!

So get off your duff right now and order, order, order! Remember it's only $29.95 and it makes a really swell gift. And whether you are a loner or love to interact with others, this is one offer that's definitely right for you.

Visit us on the World Wide Web at: www.browniepointsthebook.com. or call 1-800-852-6104. Additional copies of the book can be ordered from our website or toll-free number.

All kidding aside, this is a real honest-to-goodness offer! Allow a minimum of 6-8 weeks for delivery.

About the Author:

A cottage-dwelling humourist from the shores of Lake Erie, Brian is best known as a sit-down comic, life traveller and theorist. His formal schooling is in engineering, however real-life education comes from practicing what he preaches to his thirteen-year-old son, Spencer.

- Be kind
- Be polite
- Do your best